150 Key Concepts in
psychology

emotions

wisdom

nature

placebo

ego

What's the Difference?

id

nocebo

nurture

intelligence

moods

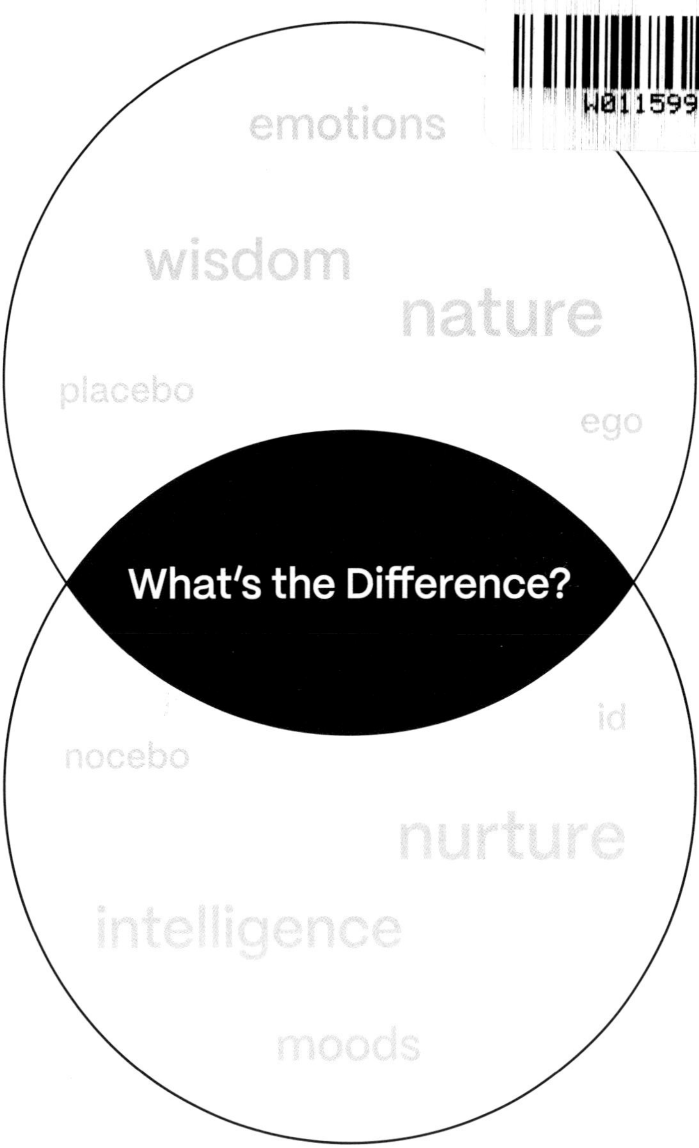

IVY PRESS

introduction

This book is part of a new series and a brand new approach to popular reference, based on the question, 'What's the difference?'. Inside you will find clear, snappy explanations of 150 paired words that make up a comprehensive, easy-to-understand psychology primer. This book is for those who want to know more about the most important, weird and wonderful ideas in psychology. The concepts are explored in pairs to help resolve common confusions and misconceptions.

What's the difference? explains 150 big-ticket psychology topics. These are subjects you might be aware of, but perhaps have not fully understood, like id and ego, dreaming and hypnosis, or slow and fast thinking. It also includes the ideas of key figures, such as Sigmund Freud and Carl Jung. We have all heard the terms and the names, but by exploring definitions in this new way, we cut to the heart of each topic quickly and clearly. This helps to avoid those all too frequent conceptual slip-ups. So, if you mix up 'stress' and 'burnout', confuse 'guilt' with 'shame', then this book is for you. Read it from cover to cover or, of course, dip in and choose concepts that spark your interest.

The book is divided up into six sections. The first sets the foundation for the rest of the book by looking at some of the most significant terms that are used in psychology, like 'behaviour' and 'cognition', 'classical' and 'operant conditioning', or 'sports psychology' and 'growth mindset'. If you are more curious about mental health and emotions, then explore section three and get to grips with resilience and neuroticism, envy and jealousy. The 'thinking, memory & perception' section, meanwhile, guides you through fascinating phenomena including colour blindness and synaesthesia, memory and forgetting.

'Therapy & theory' looks at how the study of psychology fits in with therapeutic practice. You can compare and contrast psychodynamic therapy with cognitive behavioural therapy (CBT), family with couples' therapy. All of which is useful in the current age, as there is a smorgasbord of therapeutic ideas out there.

'Social psychology' moves outwards from the individual to society and looks at amazing research, experiments and ideas regarding prejudice, contact theory, the bystander effect, and at the distinctions and overlap between love and attraction, obedience and conformity, emotional intelligence and theory of mind.

Hello brain! Our operational centre. The last section of this book is devoted to neuropsychology: what is the real difference between the mind and the brain, consciousness and the unconscious, the limbic system and the cortex? And how do we identify brain diseases like Alzheimer's and Parkinson's?

How lucky are we to have all this research and knowledge at our fingertips, helping us to understand ourselves and our environments? This book will help enrich and deepen your understanding of why we think, feel and behave in the ways we do. So, if you want to know the difference between nature and nurture, schizophrenia and psychosis, the mind and the brain, then read on.

how to use this book

Each double-page spread is designed to
make the concepts clear and accessible.
Expert text explains each key term, from
the basic idea to the nuanced concept.

Sigmund Freud

Sigmund Freud (1856–1939) revolutionized our understanding of the mind. He came up with 'the talking cure' – psychoanalysis. This was the first time in the history of Western medicine that mentally ill people were actually listened to!

Psychoanalysis was Freud's own, quirky method for treating mental 'illness'. He saw mental problems as originating from conflicts within the psyche. By listening to his patients, Freud developed theories of the working mind, creating concepts like the unconscious and psychic defence mechanisms.

There were plenty of naysayers (as there are now), who thought Freud himself had lost the plot and that his approach was damaging. Take one of his most famous cases: 'Little Hans' with a horse phobia. Freud used his own concept of the Oedipus complex – an unconscious sexual longing for the parent of the opposite sex – to explain this phobia. According to Freud's theory, Hans had displaced his fears and rivalry with his father onto horses. Through talking, he was cured. Make of that what you will! Today, cognitive behavioural therapy (CBT), not psychoanalysis, is the preferred treatment for most phobias.

There has been much controversy surrounding Freud's theories, specifically the big 'Freudian coverup'. It emerged that in developing ideas about infant sexuality, Freud was hearing stories of real sexual abuse, but the idea of adults abusing children was so shocking in that era that he changed what he heard to create the theory of infant sexuality and the Oedipus complex.

1 In a nutshell
The creator of psychoanalysis. He trained as a doctor, and later developed his interest in the talking cure as a way of healing psychological distress.

2 Why it matters
Freud's ideas have had a profound impact on our understanding of human behaviour, and influence contemporary thinking about art, literature and politics.

3 Key figures
Anna Freud, 1895–1982
Melanie Klein, 1882–1960

4 Make the connection
id/ego, pp.10–11
envy, p.82
psychodynamic therapy, p.104
the unconscious, p.147

I'm the father of psychoanalysis

Carl Jung

From around 1900, Carl Jung (1875–1961) worked closely with Freud, and it is thought that Jung looked up to the older man. Jung became a significant member of the psychoanalytic movement at that time and contributed to the growth of psychoanalytic ideas.

In around 1913, however, Jung had many theoretical disagreements with Freud, which led to a split between them. At this point Jung founded a school of his own called 'analytical psychology', similar in name to Freud's 'psychoanalytic' school, but very different.

Jung, a psychiatrist who also become an analyst, was altogether more spiritual than Freud; he felt there was much more to the psyche than id, ego and superego, and he developed the notion of the collective unconscious – a layer of consciousness shared by all human beings. The collective unconscious consists of myths, universal themes and archetypes that evoke common emotions in all of us. Examples of archetypes are the hero, the mother, anima (the feminine element of the male psyche) and animus (the masculine aspect of the female psyche). Jung suggested that archetypes give us a larger symbolic or metaphorical language, allowing us to consider people in their widest contexts. He also invented the notions of extroverted and introverted personality types, which are today in common usage.

Despite the usual criticism levelled against psychoanalytic work – an absence of empirical research, Eurocentrism and a lack of scientific validity – Jung's work influences mainstream psychology and the creative therapies.

In a nutshell
Jung was a student of Freud but broke away to develop his own branch of analytic psychology. He created the idea of the collective unconscious and personality types.

Why it matters
Jung's work has been influential in psychology, psychiatry and the study of religion, literature and the arts.

Key figures
Adolf Bastian, 1826–1903
Rowland Hazard III, 1881–1945
Andrew Samuels, b.1949

Make the connection
neuroticism, p.71
psychodynamic therapy, p.104
introversion/ extroversion, pp.120–21

The collective unconscious is the thing...

---

1 *In a nutshell* is a single-sentence summary of each concept.

2 *Why it matters* gives the context for how the concept relates to our day-to-day lives.

3 *Key figures* names those all-important folk engaged in the debate.

4 *Make the connection* helps to navigate connections across the book.

5 The illustrations offer a visual way to understand tricky ideas.

behaviour

We all know what behaviour is, don't we? But there's more to it than you might think. Psychologists nowadays think of human behaviours as the interaction between the *internal* mind and the *external* physical environment. They have studied human behaviour for years, trying to understand and even predict how we behave in various situations.

Some big-name psychologists – John Watson, Burrhus Frederik (B.F.) Skinner and Ivan Pavlov – theorized that behaviour is simply a reaction to a specific event or stimulus. Nothing more, nothing less. Skinner looked at behaviours and rewards in rats. In his 'Skinner box', rats began to hit a lever more frequently when this lever triggered the release of food pellets. Seems obvious, doesn't it? And, of course, it works for humans, too. The rewarding sugar high and delicious taste sensation of that chocolate-y dessert nearly always makes us go back for more!

Behavioural psychologists today spend their time researching consumer behaviour patterns, like how we behave around a supermarket, to make us buy more. Health psychologists also look at our behaviours, developing tricks to help us bring more exercise into our lives, for example. Think of how the 'Couch to 5k' running app builds up your stamina using daily rewards and a motivating voice. It's all in the psychology! With the rapid development of online behaviours and AI technologies, behaviour informatics is a fast-growing area of study. Psychologists are trying to catch up with the exponentially increasing data on our behaviours.

In a nutshell
Behaviours are the ways in which we act in various situations.

Why it matters
Understanding and predicting how people interact with each other and their environments can make for quicker learning and smoother lives.

Key figures
James Clear, b.1986
Ivan Pavlov. 1849–1936
B. F. Skinner, 1904–1990
Edward Thorndike, 1874–1949

Make the connection
operant/classical conditioning, pp.22–3
confirmation bias, p.48
nature/nurture, pp.116–17

I'm shopping.

cognition

The word 'cognition' comes from the Latin *cognóscere*, which means 'to know or to learn about', and the concept encompasses all aspects of our thinking and knowing. Cognitive psychology is devoted to studying how people actually think, learn and process information.

With all that humans can do, even at the simplest level, this is a pretty massive topic. There are so many things going on when we are thinking, consciously or otherwise. Think about it – we are using our attention: noticing something that is interesting or important and, at the same time, ignoring things we don't feel are significant. We are using memory – when we ride a bike without effort, for example, or even when we speak. Language and how it is learned and formed are another important part of cognition. Cognition also includes the workings of perception – how we see colours, for example – and the way in which our brains process this information. On top of all this is the concept of metacognition, which means thinking about thinking!

Following the trend towards behaviourism, it dawned on psychologists that there is more to being human than pure stimulus and response. Memories, thoughts and feelings must also influence how we behave. Nowadays, modern technology like electroencephalograms (EEGs) and functional magnetic resonance imaging (fMRIs) means that cognitive processes are more easily studied than ever before and scientists are modelling artificial intelligence (AI) on our own human cognitive processes.

In a nutshell
Refers to brain action, thinking and acquiring knowledge through experience. Cognitive psychology is concerned with these mental processes.

Why it matters
We are thinking, feeling human beings. Understanding cognition and how it works is essential if we want to live better lives. It can enhance technology, too.

Key figures
Albert Bandura, 1925–2021
Noam Chomsky, b.1928
Daniel Kahneman, 1934–2024
Lawrence Kohlberg, 1927–1987

Make the connection
confirmation bias, p.48
depression, p.89
cognitive behavioural therapy, p.105

I'm thinking of shopping.

counsellor

A counsellor is someone who is trained to give general emotional support and guidance to people facing difficulties in their lives – the death of a loved one, struggles at work, relationship issues and more.

There are many different specialities under the counselling umbrella – counselling for couples, for anxieties or depression, as well as for children and young people. Some counsellors hold a degree in a related subject, like psychology or social work, but many do not. All counsellors, however, have a specific one- to four-year training in counselling, in which they are taught to pay very close attention to exactly what clients are saying (and doing). In this wat they help their clients to grow emotionally and to find their own unique ways of navigating life. Counsellors pride themselves on being good listeners.

One of the key figures in counselling was Carl Rogers, who, in the 1950s, came up with the concept of person-centred therapy. Central to this approach is the idea of unconditional positive regard (UPR), which describes a counsellor's total acceptance of all aspects of their client's way of being. Rogers and his followers believed that people who don't have this pure and unadulterated positive acceptance in their lives hold negative beliefs about themselves. Using UPR, the counsellor will attend to all verbal and non-verbal communications that their client brings to a session. This helps people to open a window of understanding and to better manage their situation.

In a nutshell
Counsellors are trained to listen closely to people who are in emotional pain.

Why it matters
With the diminishing influence of religion and a move to more individualistic living, counselling is becoming more widespread, particularly in the West.

Key figures
Sigmund Freud, 1856–1939
Abraham Maslow, 1908–1970
Susie Orbach, b.1946
Carl Rogers, 1902–1987

Make the connection
Sigmund Freud/ Carl Jung, p.30–31
moods/emotions, pp.66–7
stress/burnout, pp.76–7
anxiety/depression, pp.88–9

clinical psychologist

It can be confusing for people outside of these professions, because clinical psychologists, psychiatrists (see p.103) and counsellors all work in the same field, but their respective trainings, and the treatments they offer, differ substantially. Psychiatrists are doctors by training and use medication to help patients in distress. Clinical psychologists are not trained in medicine and only work with the behavioural and psychological elements of distress. Counsellors usually help people with common, everyday life challenges.

Clinical psychologists deal with more complex cases and more severe psychological issues. They have around seven years of training; unlike counsellors, all clinical psychologists have an undergraduate psychology degree, followed by a doctoral training specifically in clinical psychology.

Clinical psychologists pride themselves on being scientist practitioners. This means that they consider the latest research findings to offer the most effective interventions. Many clinical psychologists also carry out their own research, individually or in teams. They work in a range of settings: hospitals, doctors' practices, psychiatric and academic institutions.

After a detailed assessment, a clinical psychologist will sometimes offer psycho-educational interventions, like relaxation techniques, or behavioural change tasks. This usually happens alongside talking therapy. They can also intervene on a wider systemic level by writing reports supporting school, work or housing requests.

In a nutshell
A scientist practitioner, who uses evidence-based research to inform their practice.

Why it matters
It is important to know what clinical psychologists do, to understand if they are the right kind of talking therapist for a particular problem.

Key figures
Albert Bandura, 1925–2021
Aaron Beck, 1921–2021
Marsha Linehan, b.1943
Martin Seligman, b.1942

Make the connection
habit/addiction, pp.86–7
cognitive behavioural therapy, p.105

id

The id does not exist physically, you cannot see it on a brain scan – it is a concept, developed by Austrian neurologist Sigmund Freud in the late 1800s. By listening to patients and drawing on his own self-analysis, Freud invented psychoanalytic theory and the 'structural' model of the human mind, which states that the mind has three main components: the id (Latin for 'it'), the ego and the superego.

Freud said that the id is the part of the mind that wants it NOW! It seeks immediate gratification, without any inhibitions. It is the most primitive and primal of the mind's psychic structures, operating unconsciously and driven by impulses that are innate in us as human animals.

The pleasure principle – the instinctive need to avoid pain and find pleasures – works through the id. Basically, the id craves pleasure, at all costs. In adults where the id is not fulfilled, negative consequences ensue. A mild example of this is the experience of being 'hangry', or angry due to hunger; our primitive feelings lead us to behave irritably and badly. Road rage is another example of the id manifesting in terms of impulsive aggression.

Freud's theory of psychic structures is often criticized as being too far-fetched and untestable, but can nevertheless be helpful as a way of viewing minds and behaviours.

In a nutshell
Part of Sigmund Freud's structural model of the human mind, the id seeks to maximize pleasure and minimize discomfort.

Why it matters
What makes us tick, and why do we react in certain ways to particular situations? Freud's notion of the id helps us to explain primitive behaviours.

Key figures
Anna Freud, 1895–1982
Sigmund Freud, 1856–1939
Melanie Klein, 1882–1960
Donald Winnicott, 1896–1971

Make the connection
dreaming/hypnosis, pp.12–13
neuroticism, p.71
envy/jealousy, pp.82–3
mind/brain, pp.154–5

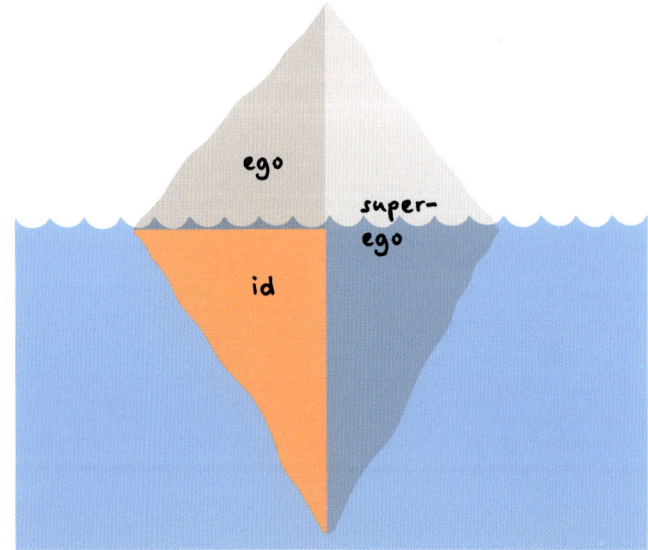

ego

Ego is Latin for 'I', and the ego is another component of Sigmund Freud's structural model of the psyche.

Nowadays the term 'ego' is so widely used that the meaning has shifted and we use the word to refer to someone who is 'all about me', arrogant and full of themselves. Originally, however, Freud's theory proposed the ego as a middleman, or mediator, in the conflict between the id and the reality of the outside world. As we grow up, we generally stop acting through the id, screaming out for food or for the toilet. According to Freud's theory, this is because our ego comes into play and seeks to find a more socially acceptable way to satisfy our needs, toileting and otherwise. In a way the ego can be thought of as the civilizing force in our human behaviours.

According to Freud's theory of the reality principle (different from the pleasure principle), the ego is situated between two conflicting forces: the id, and the need to adhere to societal ideas, which he called the superego. Freud suggested that, in order to manage this psychic conflict, the ego draws on defence mechanisms like denial, repression and rationalization. But that's another story...

The ego develops in childhood, through the influence of our parents, friendships and other wider influences, as we all learn how to function in the world. It is thought that the successful development of the ego is essential for living with ease.

In a nutshell
The mediator between id and superego in Freud's structural model of the mind.

Why it matters
The concept of the ego helps us to understand why we act the way we do and feel the way we feel.

Key figures
Erik Erikson, 1902–1994
Sigmund Freud, 1856–1961
Carl Jung, 1875–1961
Melanie Klein, 1882–1960

Make the connection
personality types/the big five, pp.114–15
nature/nurture, pp.116–17
consciousness/ the unconscious, pp.146–7

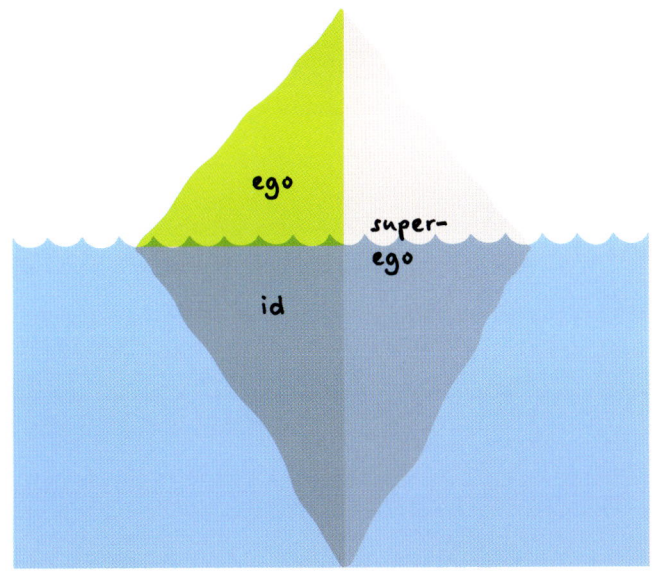

dreaming

What do dreams *really* mean? The three main theories that try to explain the rich experience of dreaming are the psychoanalytic, cognitive and neurological.

Sigmund Freud, the father of psychoanalysis, had a massive influence on the understanding of dreams, which he described as the 'royal road to the unconscious'. He felt that dreams could be used to understand repressed desires, unresolved conflicts, worries and fears. Carl Jung, a close colleague of Freud, felt dreams were our unconscious mind's way of communicating with our conscious mind. He proposed that dreams are highly symbolic, with different symbols having different meanings for different people.

Cognitive theories of dreams suggest that our dreams are a rehearsal, allowing the brain to practise and repeat the various events in our lives. Rapid Eye Movement (REM) sleep, when most dreams happen, is that phase when our eyes are moving below our eyelids. Our brainwaves show most activity during our dreams. Neurological theories of dreams focus on the brain's neural activity. A big player here is activation-synthesis or neural activation theory, the work of two twentieth-century psychiatrists, John Allan Hobson and Robert McCarley, which suggests that a dream is the mind trying to fully comprehend the neural activity occurring in the brain stem.

In short, there are many different theories that attempt to explain the complex and multifaceted phenomenon of dreaming. Which one convinces you?

In a nutshell
There are different theories as to why we have dreams and what they 'do'.

Why it matters
Not only is it fun to try and work out what our dreams represent, dreams can help us navigate our daily encounters with people and the world.

Key figures
Sigmund Freud, 1856–1939
Carl Jung, 1875–1961
Lisa Miller
Alice Robb

Make the connection
memory/forgetting, pp.40–41
emotional intelligence, p.136
the unconscious, p.147

hypnosis

Hypnosis – a state of heightened suggestibility and altered consciousness induced by a hypnotist – is pretty popular as entertainment these days: under hypnosis you might speak a foreign language or cluck like a chicken! But it can also be used for therapeutic or experimental purposes.

While both dreaming and hypnosis are altered states of consciousness, their mechanisms differ. Like dreaming, the state of hypnosis is characterized by deep relaxation, but, unlike dreaming, it involves a heightened focus and increased suggestibility.

The thoughts and perceptions of a person under hypnosis can be directed. Within a single, short session, hypnosis can change behaviours and feelings – so that the hypnotized person does indeed cluck like a chicken. Equally, though, it can have longer-lasting effects, after the session has finished, helping people to give up smoking, for example, manage compulsive behaviours like overeating, or conquer fears and anxieties. In clinical settings hypnosis is also used for pain management.

American psychologist Ernest Hilgard was a big influence on theories of hypnosis. He said when someone is hypnotized, part of the mind is separated off and the other part is like a hidden observer watching the hypnotic process at all times, so that they can observe pain, for example, without ever feeling it.

While some people believe it is all a bit 'woo woo', others argue that hypnosis is a non-invasive but powerful treatment – an effective way to achieve long-term therapeutic goals.

In a nutshell
An altered state of consciousness, of deep physical and mental relaxation with awareness.

Why it matters
Hypnosis is a valuable, non-physical intervention for a range of issues. It is a powerful treatment for pain relief, addictions and other behaviours.

Key figures
Alfred Binet, 1857–1911
Jean-Martin Charcot, 1825–1893
Ernest Hilgard, 1904–2001

Make the connection
false memories/ illusions, pp.46–7
cortex/imbic system, pp.144–5
consciousness/the unconscious, pp.146–7

neurodiversity

The concept of neurodiversity is relatively new in the world of psychology. The term was coined by Judy Singer, an Australian sociologist, in the late 1990s. The idea challenges the former medical model, which would treat conditions like autism, attention deficit hyperactivity disorder (ADHD) and dyslexia as psychologically 'abnormal'. Rather than viewing these conditions as dysfunctional, the model of neurodiversity suggests they are natural variations on the psychic norm.

The neurodiversity paradigm promotes a shared understanding of our diversity, rather than attempting to 'fix' differences between people. Therapeutically speaking, this can result in a more collaborative approach, looking at strengths rather than deficits in each of us. Psychologists working in this field, whether in research or practice, work out how to help neurodivergent people navigate their worlds through teaching them strategies and adapting their environments.

In educational settings, this has resulted in a move away from the one-size-fits-all approach to an individualized one, in which a teacher, ideally, ensures that all learning materials accommodate all types of learner.

In a nutshell

A term that refers to a range of neurological and brain conditions; it represents a move away from labelling learning and neurological difficulties as 'abnormal'.

Why it matters

Research and practice with neurodivergent people helps us to recognize that, as humans, we all vary.

Key figures

Simon Baron-Cohen, b.1958
Oswald Berkhan, 1834–1917
Georges Gilles de la Tourette, 1857–1904
Samuel Orton, 1879–1948

Make the connection

dyslexia, p.61
mental health/mental illness, pp.68–9
ASD/ADHD, pp.92–3

LGBTQ+ psychology

The LGBTQ+ community has particular needs that require psychological expertise, and in this sense LGBTQ+ psychology is similar to psychology for neurodiversity. Both promote ideas of inclusivity and resist old-fashioned ways of pathologizing, and stigmatizing, difference.

LGBTQ+ psychology deals with the unique psychological experiences of people who are gay, lesbian, bisexual, transsexual, queer or of any other non-heteronormative orientation. Members of the LGBTQ+ community experience specific anxieties, depression and mental health issues as compared to their heterosexual or cisgender (those who identify with the sex they were born in) counterparts. This area has, therefore, continued to develop.

Areas of LGBTQ+ research and practice are diverse, covering mental health, discrimination, relationships and identity formation. LGBTQ+ psychology also addresses ideas around intersectionality, where people have multiple identities that are marginalized – for example, people who are neurodivergent and also transgender.

Psychological therapeutic approaches with LGBTQ+ people are affirmative and supportive. People get psychological help to address issues around coming out, family dynamics, loss, change and growth. Potentially helpful psychological theories around coming out include Vivienne Cass's LGBTQ identity formation model and Anthony D'Augelli's model of sexual identity disclosure.

In a nutshell
The field has developed in recent years to understand the specific needs and psychological growth of this diverse community.

Why it matters
With a greater understanding of all groups of society, we can promote better understanding in diverse communities.

Key figures
Edward Carpenter, 1844–1929
Karl Ulrichs, 1825–1895, and Magnus Hirschfeld, 1868–1935

Make the connection
love/attraction, pp.128–9
loneliness/solitude, pp.132–3
prejudice/contact theory, pp.138–9
mind/brain, pp.154–5

creativity

Whose are the first names that come to mind when you think of creativity? Leonardo Da Vinci, Marie Curie, Oprah Winfrey? These people broke free from the constraints of the mainstream to create incredible new things. From life-changing inventions to everyday problem-solving, creativity is to do with how humans generate original ideas, objects and experiences. It is, perhaps, the thing that really makes us human.

Psychologists have come up with different theories to explain human creativity. One of these is Teresa Amabile's componential model of creativity, widely used by workplace psychologists in helping managers enhance creativity in their teams. Amabile suggests that there are three essential components to the creative process: expertise, creative thinking skills and intrinsic motivation. If we apply the model to a situation not typically thought of as 'creative' – something like a government department – we can understand the process more clearly. A government department needs to create new policies – the team needs expertise about what is needed and why. They use creative thinking skills to work out the best solutions with imagination and perseverance. Finally, the team needs motivation – an inner passion for coming up with new solutions. Voila! a model for how creativity works.

In a nutshell
Theories of creativity explain how we make literature, music and art, and also how we come up with new ideas in other fields.

Why it matters
Part of what makes us human is this special skill of creativity; it is worth knowing how it works and how we can harness its power.

Key figures
Mihaly Csikszentmihalyi, 1934–2021
Dennis Kinney
Adolphe Quetelet, 1796–1874
Ruth Richards

Make the connection
dreaming, p.12
synesthaesia, p.52
hallucinations, p.63
flow states/ psychedelic trips, pp.96—7

willpower

Inventor Thomas Edison said that creative genius is 1 per cent inspiration and 99 per cent perspiration. Great accomplishments depend on hard work as much as they do on great ideas. Time to think about willpower, which involves the ability to exert self-control, resist impulses and regulate our emotions to achieve long-term goals, despite challenges along the way.

Currently there are three main models of willpower in psychology. The ego depletion model says that willpower is a limited resource and can simply run out. If you keep on resisting temptations, eventually your capacity for that self-control will be exhausted.

The strength model proposed by Roy Baumeister, on the other hand, suggests that willpower is like a muscle – the more you use it the stronger it gets. This theory has it that repeated small acts of self-control can lead to more robust willpower over time. Use it or lose it!

Thirdly, personal enjoyment and interest are really big factors in maintaining willpower. The expectancy-value theory tells us that people are more likely to use willpower if there is a reward at the end. Go on and promise yourself that bacon butty afterwards and you are more likely to make the trip out to the gym!

In a nutshell
The ability to show self-control and perseverance.

Why it matters
Willpower and self-control affect everything we do individually and in the context of a civilized society. How can we execute our plans for the future, if we can't see them through?

Key figures
Roy Baumeister, b.1953
Martin Hagger
Diane Tice

Make the connection
classical/operant conditioning, pp.22–3
growth mindset, p.32
habit/addiction, pp.86–7
mind/brain, pp.154–5

placebo effect

A placebo may look like medicine, but it's not the real deal, more like an intentional fake! The term 'placebo' (from the Latin meaning 'I shall please') actually originated in clinical studies. Scientists trialling medications on patients would give a genuine treatment to one group and a placebo – for example, a sugar pill – to the other group, and then examine recovery in both. Researchers realized that the people who had received the sugar pill got a lot better, too. This came to be known as the placebo effect – the phenomenon whereby people with symptoms are given fake medication and the symptoms improve, even though the treatment itself has no therapeutic benefits. In 1955 the American anesthesiologist Henry K. Beecher wrote a paper called 'The Powerful Placebo' and since then it has been considered a scientific fact.

The placebo effect occurs in all kinds of people, with a range of different conditions. We see it in cases of pain management, psychiatric disorders and various immune responses. It is real and observable; scientists can see changes in heart rate, blood pressure and hormonal activity in patients who have taken a placebo. This, of course, has many implications for medical care and research.

There are a number of factors that can explain the phenomenon. An expectation effect, where the patient believes that a pill will work, can trigger a release of chemicals that lead to improvements in symptoms. Learning theory is also used to explain how we come to associate a specific pill with healing feelings and so healing happens.

In a nutshell
Describes how a patient's symptoms can improve after taking 'fake' or non-therapeutic medicine.

Why it matters
Smoother recovery and reduced medication costs are among the possible implications of considering placebo healing when treating sick people.

Key figures
Henry Beecher, 1904–1976
E. Morton Jellinek, 1890–1963

Make the connection
behaviour/cognition, pp.6–7
memory/forgetting, pp.40–41
brainwashing, p.42

nocebo effect

Why do so many people immediately throw away the unread side-effects leaflet when opening a new packet of medicine? They don't want to be influenced by negative expectations. They are trying to avoid the nocebo effect. This is the opposite of the placebo effect and happens when a person anticipates negative reactions to a drug or treatment and then actually experiences that harm – someone who experiences a nocebo effect will take a neutral sugar pill and still feel awful in response to it.

At the heart of the nocebo effect is a person's negative anticipation: 'This treatment is going to hurt!' This feeling is thought to trigger physiological responses that are then in keeping with their expectations. The nocebo effect leads to elevated anxiety and fear, which can lead to physiological stress responses in the body – the release of the stress hormone cortisol, increased heart rate and temperature – all of which worsen symptoms.

The phenomenon was noticed (and named – 'nocebo' comes from the Latin meaning 'I shall harm') when researchers found that people reported negative symptoms even when they were given fake treatments. The scientists concluded that this reaction was simply due to patients holding negative expectations.

It is important for researchers to pay attention to both placebo and nocebo effects in medical trial studies. There is a clear interplay between the psychological and the physical, between mind and body, which can help or hinder clinical research and practice.

In a nutshell
Happens when a patient expects to feel unwell after taking medicine and does, even though the medicine was fake.

Why it matters
It is crucial to know about the interplay between mind and body and how this can impact our health and treatments.

Key figures
Michael Bernstein
Charlotte Blease
Bessel van der Kolk, b.1943

Make the connection
habit/addiction, pp.86–7
brain scans/electro-encephalography, pp.150–51
mind/brain, pp.154–5

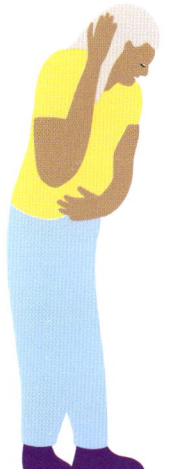

phrenology

In the late eighteenth century, phrenology was all the rage. Rather like a primitive precursor to neuroscience, it was a way to categorize sections of the brain, matching them to personality traits, intelligence and character. Phrenologists argued that the way to do this was through examining the lumps and bumps of the human skull. Practitioners like Franz Joseph Gall, a German physician, and his colleague Johann Spurzheim said that they could identify personality traits like kindness, musical talent and even the love of children through feeling contours on the head.

Scientists and lay people were fascinated by this new 'science'. Phrenologists travelled the West giving lectures, and phrenological societies were established to share ideas.

As technology improved, however, and neurology developed through more sophisticated methods like brain dissection and neuroimaging, phrenology fell into disrepute. It was criticized for being too simplistic and for making unfounded claims. The basic idea that distinct brain regions are associated with specific functions is valid, but phrenology has been replaced by more nuanced, sophisticated and evidence-based approaches in neuroscience.

One of the lessons that research psychologists have gained from this wave of pseudoscience is always to engage in scientific rigour, critical thinking and empirical evidence before shouting about new approaches.

In a nutshell
A largely discredited pseudoscience. It suggested that the formation of the skull and the brain underneath could be matched to personality traits.

Why it matters
Particular ideas grasp the imagination and it is interesting to consider why, as well as studying how scientific theories are developed over time.

Key figures
Pierre Paul Broca, 1824–1880
Franz Joseph Gall, 1758–1828
Johann Spurzheim, 1776–1832

Make the connection
neuroplasticity, p.27
traits, p.112
brain scans/electro-encephalography, pp.150–51

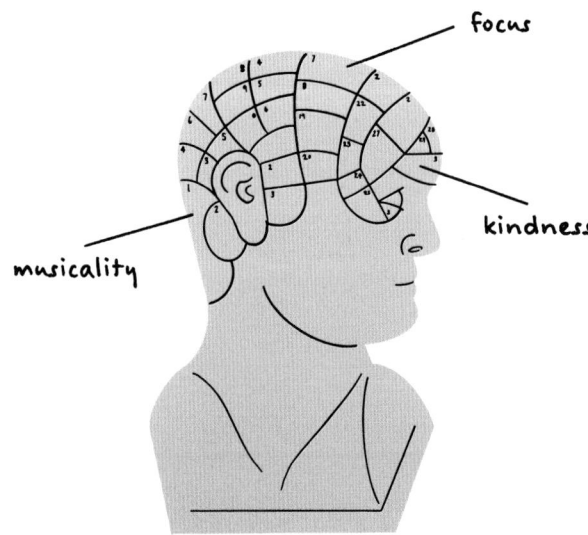

focus

kindness

musicality

physiognomy

Like phrenology, the pseudoscience of physiognomy was based on the look and shape of a person's features. But physiognomy is the interpretation of a person's character based solely on their facial characteristics.

The approach originated in Ancient Greece and China. Aristotle, the Ancient Greek philosopher, linked certain character traits with specific facial features. A classic example was the idea that physically having a high brow meant that a person had an affinity for the arts and culture – we still use the phrase 'high brow' today. Ancient China also played a role in the history of this idea; traditional practitioners in Chinese medicine would often examine facial features to diagnose health conditions and predict destiny.

Physiognomy experienced a resurgence in popularity during the European Renaissance, when the Swiss philosopher Johann Kaspar Lavater argued that the study of facial features could reveal deep insights into a person's moral worth. He was followed in the nineteenth century by Cesare Lombroso, an Italian criminologist who linked physiognomy to his own theories of criminal anthropology. He believed that certain features of the face and skull could identify those predisposed to criminal behaviour.

Physiognomy, like phrenology, was dismissed by the scientific community because of the lack of rigour and evidence to support it. The rise of empirical psychology meant that physiognomy was increasingly viewed as quackery.

In a nutshell
A popular scientific discipline in centuries past, physiognomy suggests a person's character can be predicted from their facial features.

Why it matters
It is interesting to learn from historical scientific theories and see how they impact on today's thinking, while wondering how much of today's 'science' will, at some point, be cast into a dustbin of disbelief.

Key figures
Gary Klein, b.1944
Johann Kaspar Lavater, 1741–1801
Cesare Lombroso, 1835–1909

Make the connection
dissociative identity disorder, p.99
traits/social roles, pp.112–13
lateralization, p.149

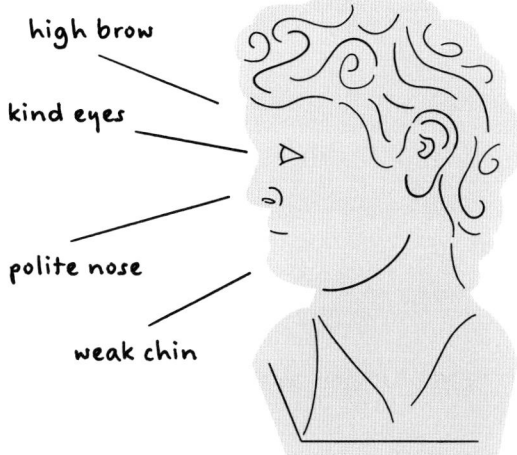

high brow

kind eyes

polite nose

weak chin

classical conditioning

AKA, learning by association! This is a key concept in psychology, first studied by Russian physiologist Ivan Pavlov in the late nineteenth and early twentieth centuries.

In Pavlov's famous experiments, dogs were presented with an edible treat (which he called the unconditioned stimulus, UCS) at the sound of a bell. When the food was presented to the dog, it dribbled in anticipation and Pavlov called this saliva production the unconditioned response (UCR). Over many repetitions Pavlov's dogs learned to associate the bell with food, so that, eventually, the sound of the bell alone, with no food, would cause the dogs to salivate (the bell has become a conditioned stimulus, CS, eliciting a conditioned response, CR). This is the original process of classical conditioning as discovered by Pavlov.

There are all kinds of knock-on effects connected with classical conditioning, like generalization (a dog might salivate for a different bell tone), or extinction (a bell is rung repeatedly without the dog having any food – eventually the salivation will stop).

Outside the laboratory, classical conditioning can be used to explain lots of behaviours. A young child going to school meets their warm and nurturing teacher (UCS), who makes the child feel connected (UCR). The child associates going to school (CS) with the teacher. Going to school makes the child feel connected (CR). Classical conditioning is a useful concept for many walks of life. It is used in therapy, behaviour change, parenting training and even advertising.

In a nutshell
When two stimuli are paired in your mind – a ringing bell and food, for example – classical conditioning has occurred.

Why it matters
Knowing what from outside our own minds can influence our behaviours is useful in understanding learning of all kinds.

Key figures
Ivan Pavlov, 1849–1936
Jean Piaget, 1896–1980
B. F. Skinner, 1904–1990

Make the connection
confirmation bias, p.48
obsessive compulsive disorder, p.90
cognitive behavioural therapy, p.105

bell = food

operant conditioning

Like classical conditioning, operant conditioning connects learning and behaviours, but here the key concepts are reward and punishment, rather than stimulus–response reinforcement. Operant conditioning was studied and developed by the psychologist and behaviourist Burrhus Frederic (B. F.) Skinner (see p.6).

Skinner devised the 'operant conditioning chamber', or what is now known as the Skinner box. This was like a little laboratory for rats or pigeons and was used to test out specific hypotheses. The pigeon inside the box would learn to respond to sound stimuli to earn a reward. This reward could be positively reinforcing, such as food, or negatively reinforcing, like the removal of a noxious smell. As we might expect, Skinner proved that punishment reduced behaviours. He defined positive punishment as when we are presented with a nasty stimulus, like being beaten with a cane! Negative punishment is when a nice stimulus is removed, like taking away a child's favourite cuddly toy.

Intermittent reinforcement can be a powerful way to shape behaviour. Sometimes the animal in the box would be rewarded for their behaviours and at other times not. Intermittent reinforcement keeps the behaviour going for longer, due to the unpredictability of the reward. Slot machines, online gambling, gaming and dating websites are great examples of how intermittent reinforcement keeps a user hooked and coming back for more.

In a nutshell
Concerns rewards and punishments: an association is made between behaviours and consequences that changes behavioural patterns.

Why it matters
It can help us grown-ups (and our children) behave differently and shift unwanted habits.

Key figures
Ivan Pavlov, 1849–1936
B. F. Skinner, 1904–1990
Edward Thorndike, 1874–1949

Make the connection
cognitive reappraisal, p.65
habit/addiction, pp.86–7

food = reward

developmental psychology

This branch of psychology explores the dynamic process of human growth – how we turn from a newborn into a (hopefully) fully formed adult!

Perhaps the most important figure in developmental psychology was Swiss psychologist Jean Piaget (see p.36). He suggested that there were four key stages for all human development:

- the *sensorimotor* stage (birth to age two years), in which infants explore the world through their senses;

- the *preoperational* stage (around age two years), when a child begins to learn to speak;

- the *concrete operational* stage (seven to eleven years), when children can think for themselves and manipulate information, by counting, adding up and subtracting, for example; and

- the *formal operational* stage (eleven to sixteen years and upward), in which we use abstract thinking.

American psychologist Lawrence Kohlberg was big in this field in the 1970s and '80s, exploring our understanding of morality and capacity for ethical decision-making. Other developmental psychology theories, like those of the British psychologist John Bowlby, consider attachment in infancy and how this influences relationships later in life. Erik Erikson (se p.37), a Danish-German-American psychoanalyst, said that phases of growth across the lifespan depended on the resolution of existential crises.

In a nutshell
Has expanded our knowledge about the cognitive, emotional and social areas of human growth.

Why it matters
Developmental psychology gives us insights into our key influences and most critical periods of growth.

Key figures
Mary Ainsworth, 1913–1999
Erik Erikson, 1902–1994
Jean Piaget, 1896–1980

Make the connection
Jean Piaget/Erik Erikson, pp.36–7
twins, p.118

educational psychology

If your child were to see an educational psychologist (EP), the treatment would probably go something like this ... The psychologist would take a detailed history of your child's development, and past and present concerns at school and outside. Following this they might carry out a detailed learning assessment, including IQ tests and other reading, writing, language and learning tests over a few sessions. Classroom observations might help with this process. Following all of this an EP would make recommendations for direct interventions, including help and support in the classroom and in other environments. These recommendations might involve occupational therapists, social workers, speech and language therapists, play therapists and other professionals to help your child function to the best of their ability in a school setting.

Like clinical psychologists, EPs conduct research into innovative ways of helping children and young people. Perhaps the key aspect of educational psychology is the use of evidence-based strategies to enhance effective learning and curriculum design for children and their teachers.

While there is some overlap between developmental and educational psychology theory, the two are quite distinct when it comes to application. Educational psychologists work in schools, colleges and other learning environments. They apply psychological theory to educational practice to get the best learning out of children. In order to do this fully, they also advise and train educators.

In a nutshell
The branch of psychology concerned with the scientific study of and interventions in human learning.

Why it matters
Educational psychology helps both teachers and students to reach their potential in educational situations.

Key figures
Jerome Bruner, 1915–2016
Johann Herbart, 1776–1841
William James, 1842–1910

Make the connection
clinical psychology, p.9
resilience, p.70
family therapy, p.106

cross-cultural psychology

Psychology as an academic discipline evolved in Europe and Northern America. In more recent years psychologists across the world have started to realize that these Western, Eurocentric concepts may not be applicable in cultures with different values and belief systems. They have found that the same experiments carried out in different cultures can lead to very different outcomes. The conclusion: psychological concepts cannot necessarily be 'exported'.

Cross-cultural psychology vastly expanded from the 1960s. With the growth of globalization, notions of cultural diversity are built into most research projects, to account for the ways in which culture influences psychological function in areas like cognition, behaviour and emotions.

A clear example of the ways culture and behaviour interact is a study, conducted by Tanya Luhrmann and colleagues in 2015, with people who experience hearing voices. Californians described their voices as intrusive and unreal. In Southern India, however, voices were described as helpful, giving guidance, while in West Africa, they were described as both powerful and morally good. Another example is the 'Big Five' model of personality traits as defined by American psychologists – extroversion, agreeableness, conscientiousness, neuroticism and openness to experience – which cannot be accurately transposed to other cultures.

The conclusion? Perhaps there is no universal structure of personality because different cultures show different significant traits.

In a nutshell
Examines different psychological phenomena across the world.

Why it matters
In theory and practice, psychology can be made richer by looking at all kinds of cultural difference.

Key figures
Jefferson Fish
Margaret Mead, 1901–1978
Wilhelm Wundt, 1832–1980

Make the connection
classical/operant conditioning, pp.22–3
social Identity/birds of a feather, pp.142–3

Culture influences psychology.

neuroplasticity

In the realm of psychology, few discoveries have ignited as much excitement as the concept of neuroplasticity. Whereas cross-cultural psychology deals with human behaviour in its widest, societal context, neuroplasticity concerns minute detail of activity that goes on deep within the brain and affects our behaviours and learning.

The brain has a remarkable ability to reorganize itself, forming new neural connections in response to learning, experience and even injury. Scientists used to believe that our brains were static and unchangeable after a certain age, but recent discoveries about neuroplasticity reveal that the brain changes shape and form, like plastic, over the course of a lifetime.

Imagine the brain as a vast network of interconnected highways, with each neuron representing a junction. Neuroplasticity is like the construction of new roads and also, even, the rerouting of existing ones. Neuroplasticity allows information to flow more efficiently, enabling new skills and behaviours to emerge. Whether it's mastering a musical instrument, recovering from a stroke or overcoming trauma, neuroplasticity is at work, reshaping the brain's landscape in response to our actions and experiences.

The field of psychology is constantly evolving, with new discoveries, even whole new disciplines, emerging over time. As with cross-cultural psychology, the study of neuroplasticity has shown us how much more there is still to know about the brain and mind, and encourages us to question our preconceptions about both.

In a nutshell
The brain's inherent capacity to grow, adapt and change to allow new information to flow effectively.

Why it matters
Understanding neuroplasticity offers hope for all of us grappling with ageing brains, neurological disorders or injuries.

Key figures
Elizabeth Gould, b.1962
Eric Kandel, b.1929
Michael Merzenich, b.1942

Make the connection
cognition, p.7
depression, p.89

Our brains can change and adapt.

humanistic psychology

This school of psychology emerged first in the 1950s as part of a backlash against both psychoanalysis and behaviourism, and has gone on to influence all approaches to counselling and therapy, as well as other areas of social science, like education and economics. Abraham Maslow's 'hierarchy of needs' model forms a foundation for humanistic approaches. It proposes that humans have an innate predisposition to fulfil their greatest potential; the term he developed for this was 'self-actualization'. Unlike the psychoanalytic approach that came before, which focuses on deficits in personality and functioning, the humanistic approach focuses on positives.

One of the essential principles of this approach is encouraging self-awareness and self-reflexivity to help people change their states of minds, creating healthier, more productive selves. 'Holism' is a nice concept, to do with the holistic nature of human experience and personal agency – the capacity we all have to make our own choices and exercise our own free will – and it is also key to this approach.

Perhaps the most important therapeutic element of humanistic psychology is Carl Rogers' notion of unconditional positive regard: acceptance, empathy and valuing people without judgement to create a supportive environment for personal growth.

While humanism has had enormous influence, its critics argue that it lacks empirical rigour compared to other therapeutic approaches such as cognitive behavioural therapy (CBT) or behaviourism.

In a nutshell
Emphasizes the study of the whole person. Humanistic psychologists see the world through the eyes of their clients, rather than as external expert observers.

Why it matters
Humanistic psychology removes the stigma attached to therapy and makes it a more equal relationship, that of two people journeying together.

Key figures
Abraham Maslow, 1908–1970
Rollo May, 1909–1994
Carl Rogers, 1902–1987

Make the connection
mental health, p.68
resilience, p.70
flow states, p.96

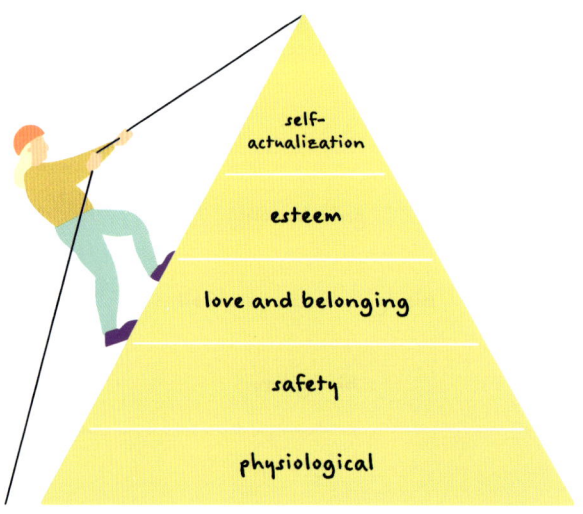

self-actualization

esteem

love and belonging

safety

physiological

positive psychology

Both humanism and positive psychology centre on the positive aspects of being human. Positive psychology looks at what is right with you rather than what is wrong, focusing on the positive aspects of human experience like feel-good emotions, strengths and virtues, values, purpose, flow and resilience.

American psychologist Martin Seligman is the founder of Western positive psychology (these ideas have been around in Eastern cultures for centuries). Since the global Covid-19 pandemic, there has been a great surge of interest in positive psychology and wellbeing thinking across the world.

In practice, positive psychologists recommend expanding windows of good feeling and joy through simple methods like journaling, meditation and developing gratitude. Random acts of kindness, like doing good deeds for others, have also been shown to help with balancing mental health These practices can take place in the therapy room, but also in educational and corporate settings.

Critics say that positive psychology oversimplifies the complexity of our behaviours and our internal psyche. They argue that there is a fundamental problem with this approach, in that positive psychology continues to individualize human distress, rather than looking at the wider context and the ways in which factors like poverty and oppression can actually create poor mental health.

In a nutshell
The scientific study and practice of human flourishing, wellbeing and happiness.

Why it matters
Moving beyond psychological deficits and towards understanding resilience and what makes for happier people might help us to create a less hostile environment and less stressed people.

Key figures
Mihaly Csikszentmihalyi, 1934–2021
Carol Dweck, b.1946
Martin Seligman, b.1942

Make the connection
emotions, p.67
hedonism, p.73
psychedelic trips, p.97

self-actualization

esteem

love and belonging

safety

physiological

Sigmund Freud

Sigmund Freud (1856–1939) revolutionized our understanding of the mind. He came up with 'the talking cure' – psychoanalysis. This was the first time in the history of Western medicine that mentally ill people were actually listened to!

Psychoanalysis was Freud's own, quirky method for treating mental 'illness'. He saw mental problems as originating from conflicts within the psyche. By listening to his patients, Freud developed theories of the working mind, creating concepts like the unconscious and psychic defence mechanisms.

There were plenty of naysayers (as there are now), who thought Freud himself had lost the plot and that his approach was damaging. Take one of his most famous cases: 'Little Hans' with a horse phobia. Freud used his own concept of the Oedipus complex – an unconscious sexual longing for the parent of the opposite sex – to explain this phobia. According to Freud's theory, Hans had displaced his fears and rivalry with his father onto horses. Through talking, he was cured. Make of that what you will! Today, cognitive behavioural therapy (CBT), not psychoanalysis, is the preferred treatment for most phobias.

There has been much controversy surrounding Freud's theories, specifically the big 'Freudian coverup'. It emerged that in developing ideas about infant sexuality, Freud was hearing stories of real sexual abuse, but the idea of adults abusing children was so shocking in that era that he changed what he heard to create the theory of infant sexuality and the Oedipus complex.

In a nutshell
The creator of psychoanalysis. He trained as a doctor, and later developed his interest in the talking cure as a way of healing psychological distress.

Why it matters
Freud's ideas have had a profound impact on our understanding of human behaviour, and influence contemporary thinking about art, literature and politics.

Key figures
Anna Freud, 1895–1982
Melanie Klein, 1882–1960

Make the connection
id/ego, pp.10–11
envy, p.82
psychodynamic therapy, p.104
the unconscious, p.147

I'm the father of psychoanalysis.

Carl Jung

From around 1900, Carl Jung (1875–1961) worked closely with Freud, and it is thought that Jung looked up to the older man. Jung became a significant member of the psychoanalytic movement at that time and contributed to the growth of psychoanalytic ideas.

In around 1913, however, Jung had many theoretical disagreements with Freud, which led to a split between them. At this point Jung founded a school of his own called 'analytical psychology', similar in name to Freud's 'psychoanalytic' school, but very different.

Jung, a psychiatrist who also become an analyst, was altogether more spiritual than Freud; he felt there was much more to the psyche than id, ego and superego, and he developed the notion of the collective unconscious – a layer of consciousness shared by all human beings. The collective unconscious consists of myths, universal themes and archetypes that evoke common emotions in all of us. Examples of archetypes are the hero, the mother, anima (the feminine element of the male psyche) and animus (the masculine aspect of the female psyche). Jung suggested that archetypes give us a larger symbolic or metaphorical language, allowing us to consider people in their widest contexts. He also invented the notions of extroverted and introverted personality types, which are today in common usage.

Despite the usual criticism levelled against psychoanalytic work – an absence of empirical research, Eurocentricism and a lack of scientific validity – Jung's work influences mainstream psychology and the creative therapies.

In a nutshell
Jung was a student of Freud but broke away to develop his own branch of analytic psychology. He created the idea of the collective unconscious and personality types.

Why it matters
Jung's work has been influential in psychology, psychiatry and the study of religion, literature and the arts.

Key figures
Adolf Bastian, 1826–1903
Rowland Hazard III, 1881–1945
Andrew Samuels, b.1949

Make the connection
neuroticism, p.71
psychodynamic therapy, p.104
introversion/ extroversion, pp.120–21

The collective unconscious is the thing...

growth mindset

American psychologist Carol Dweck coined the term 'growth mindset' in the 1980s. It emerged from years of research by Dweck and her team in schools across the USA. Dweck argued that through having a growth mindset, we develop new abilities. This happens, she says, through hard work, practice and relearning time and again. She contrasted the growth mindset with a fixed mindset, in which basic abilities, talents and intelligence are considered fixed and beyond alteration.

Growth mindset turns convention on its head: failure can now equal success, as people with this mindset see setbacks as learning opportunities. Therein lies a virtuous cycle of learning, failing and learning more! Great for worried schoolkids who don't like getting it wrong. Getting it wrong means you can learn for next time.

More recent research into neuroplasticity goes hand-in-hand with the growth mindset theory. Neuroscientists have found that learning through practice enhances our neural connectivity – i.e., neural pathways in our brain are strengthened by repetition.

Schools and colleges are now starting to teach their students about learning to learn through the growth mindset. Some, however, argue that this push is yet another way to penalize children for not trying hard enough. In a large, randomized, UK schools-based control trial, students who had received growth mindset training did not perform any better than those who had not. On top of this, the constant pass-fail assessments in education systems detract from any benefits gained through the growth mindset mentality.

In a nutshell
In the growth mindset, hard work and an openness to new experience lead to improved abilities, resilience and a love of knowledge.

Why it matters
This optimistic theory is often used in schools, universities and businesses. The take–away: it is never too late to change!

Key figures
Brené Brown, b.1965
Carol Dweck, b.1946
Michael Merzenich, b.1942

Make the connection
willpower, p.17
positive psychology, p.29

I want to win!

sports psychology

Sports psychologists examine how psychological factors affect performance and how performance can affect psychological factors in the sportsperson. The field took on its current form in the 1960s. Since then it has been fully recognized as an interdisciplinary science, drawing on knowledge from other physical sciences like physiology and biomechanics.

In 2018, Gareth Southgate, then manager of the England football team, drew on the expertise of sports psychologist Pippa Grange to help navigate setbacks, manage the pressure of taking penalties, build trust between players and manage expectations in the World Cup Tournament that year. It was considered a radical move, but served the team well!

Sports psychologists often teach cognitive behavioural skills to players working on their beliefs around success and failure, identity, losing, usefulness, stress and more. These beliefs may link to the present, to previous competitions or even back to childhood. They also try and help players to cultivate mental skills such as resilience, focus and emotional self-regulation through visualization techniques, goal-setting and positive self-talk.

Sports psychologists work with players, but also with the wider organizational system of sport – team managers or coaches – to best help them help their teams. Growth mindset theory is one part of their arsenal of skills and techniques.

In a nutshell
Sports psychology uses psychological research, theory and skill to address performance and wellbeing in sports teams.

Why it matters
Mental and physical health, as well as performance, can be enhanced by implementing the theory and method of sports psychology.

Key figures
Timothy Gallwey, b.1938
Coleman Griffith, 1893–1966
John F. Murray, 1927–2020

Make the connection
neuroplasticity, p.27
Dunning–Kruger effect, p.49
resilience, p.70

self-talk

Self-talk is the way you talk to yourself, your inner voice. Although it is connected to neurolinguistic programming (NLP), it is just one small component of the technique – NLP encompasses many more psychological elements.

Understanding the process of self-talk and intrapersonal communication is important for managing mental health. This is because self-talk can deeply affect your self-image and beliefs about yourself. It can influence decision-making and it impacts on your responses to situations. In psychology, particularly in the field of cognitive behavioural therapy (CBT), negative self-talk is often linked to anxiety, stress and depression. Psychologists and therapists help people to become more aware of their negative self-talk patterns and challenge their over-critical judgements. Once the harsh negative inner voice is acknowledged, more positive self-talk can flourish.

Positive affirmations are a key component of positive self-talk. They can reprogram the unconscious mind and reduce negative self-talk and beliefs. To encourage positive self-talk, psychologists advise leaving positive messages around your room, to embed these ideas into your neural pathways. Get some labels and give it a go!

It's a two-way street: the way we talk to ourselves affects our behaviours, and our behaviours can affect our self-talk. Adopting a growth mindset can help to overcome negative self-talk, as can self-compassion and mindfulness, which help us observe our own self-talk without getting overly engaged in our negative narratives.

In a nutshell
Self-talk plays a crucial role in personal development and mental wellbeing. Your inner dialogue shapes your thoughts and behaviours.

Why it matters
We all have a constant inner voice. It is useful to be aware of what it is saying so that we can work on it and, if necessary, improve our state of mind.

Key figures
Thomas M. Brinthaupt
Alain Morin
Lev Vygotsky, 1896–1934

Make the connection
resilience, p.70
cognitive behavioural therapy, p.105

neurolinguistic programming

Oprah Winfrey, Robbie Williams and Sophie Dahl are just a few of the many celebrities who swear by the power of NLP, a technique used in personal growth, self-development and coaching contexts. It explores the connection between neurological, linguistic and behavioural processes and patterns. Developed in the 1970s by Richard Bandler and John Grinder, it was used at that time as a model to help practitioners replicate the behavioural patterns of successful people. The approach has been adopted by some therapists and also by corporations and other official bodies.

NLP works through a whole host of techniques and behavioural 'hacks', like modelling, where you spend time with people who you admire or want to be like. Mirroring is another technique, in which body language is used to make instant connections with others: when you're talking to someone, match your body language and energy level to theirs. This often happens automatically, but being aware of it can make an interaction more beneficial for you.

NLP can be used to treat problems like phobias, depression and anxieties. Proponents say that this can be done in a single session, arguing that it is a highly valuable method. Critics feel that there is no such thing as a neurological quick fix and that NLP is a pseudoscience. Can imagining not smoking and repeatedly planting negative cigarette-related words and images really make you give up?

In a nutshell
A widely used psychological approach – a way of changing someone's thoughts and behaviours to help them achieve what they want.

Why it matters
NLP helps people with their communication, confidence, self–awareness and leadership abilities.

Key figures
Richard Bandler, b.1950
John Grinder, b.1940
Virginia Satir, 1916–1988

Make the connection
dreaming/hypnosis, pp.12–13
brainwashing/mind reading, pp.42–3

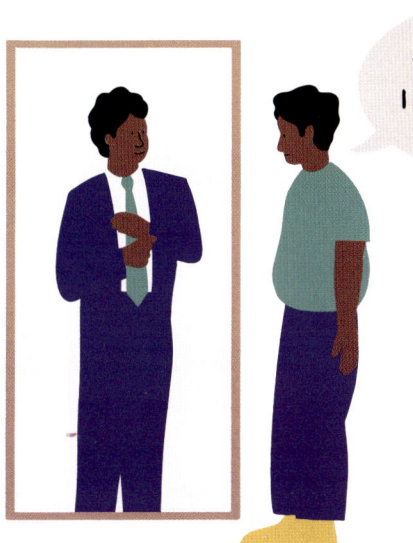

That's who I want to be!

Jean Piaget

Probably the most influential figure in developmental psychology, Jean Piaget (1896–1980) was fascinated by both biology and epistemology, the study of knowledge. So interested, in fact, that he secured two PhDs – Dr Dr Piaget! In 1918 he received a PhD in zoology from the University of Neuchâtel in Switzerland, and later one in psychology from the University of Zurich.

Piaget's most significant work came out of hundreds of observations of children, from which he formulated his Stage Theory of Cognitive Development, which proposes that all of us must progress through four key stages of development before we reach adulthood.

Piaget found that very young children, when shown a row of seven squares and then seven circles, knew that there were the same number of items in each set. When you stop and think, this is a complex task of sorting and categorizing – circles, squares, numbers, judgement. Piaget was an early contributor to understanding when and how this knowledge develops.

You can't really say the name Piaget without mentioning his peer Lev Vygotsky, whose socio-cultural theory of development was a major influence in the fields of psychology and education. Vygotsky argued that we learn through social interactions and that culture shapes our cognition. Critics say that Piaget's theories are Eurocentric and that cognitive development is more fluid than he proposed. Nevertheless, his work has had a profound impact on psychology, education and child-development practices worldwide.

In a nutshell
The first developmental psychologist to address children's development and their acquisition of knowledge and thinking abilities.

Why it matters
Piaget's theories have enriched our understanding of how children construct new knowledge.

Key figures
Alison Gopnik, b.1955
Lawrence Kohlberg, 1927–1987
Lev Vygotsky, 1896–1934

Make the connection
developmental/ educational psychology, pp.24–5
dyslexia, p.61

Childhood development is formative.

Erik Erikson

Like Piaget, Erik Erikson (1902–1994) made lasting contributions to theories of human development. He was born in Frankfurt in Germany and, unusually for the time, was raised by a single mother. In the 1920s he studied art and teaching. He was later drawn to the study of psychoanalysis and trained at the Vienna Psychoanalytic Institute. In 1933 he began working at Harvard University as a researcher and, at the same time, began a postgraduate doctoral degree in psychology (though he didn't complete this). He moved on to Yale University and the University of California, Berkeley, to follow his research interests and worked in private practice.

Erikson blended his knowledge of psychoanalysis with his interest in human development to create the theory of psychosocial development. Like Piaget's theory, Erikson's is defined by stages. It states that the development of personality depends directly on the resolution of eight crises through the life cycle: for example, trust versus mistrust, intimacy versus isolation, and integrity versus despair. Erikson's eight-stage theory encompasses the later years, beyond childhood. Failure to complete each stage leads to an unhealthy sense of self: for example, if we are struggling with intimacy in our relationships (stage 6 in Erikson's model), we may regress to stage 5 (identity vs. role confusion) and find ourselves grappling with sense of self. Failing to successfully navigate stage 6, according to the model, means we may never develop meaningful connections with others. We would need help from ourselves or another to move on to the next stage.

In a nutshell
Developed the psychosocial theory of development. He said that in order to achieve a balanced personality, a person must successfully resolve a series of conflicts.

Why it matters
Despite criticisms concerning his theory's empirical validity and cultural specificity, it has had an enduring impact on the ways we see the world.

Key figures
Lawrence Kohlberg, 1927–1987
James Marcia, 1937–1965
Margaret Mead, 1901–1978

Make the connection
wisdom, p.45
cognitive reserve, p.59
emotional intelligence, p.136

Each life stage leads on to the next.

slow thinking

Psychologist and popular author Daniel Kahneman, in his 2012 book *Thinking Fast and Slow*, says that there are two modes of thought: system 1, fast, instinctive and emotional thinking; system 2, slower, deliberate and more logical thinking. He suggests that we can all improve the way we make decisions by deliberately slowing down our thinking – making it more conscious and effortful. According to Kahneman, slow thinking happens using system 2, which engages the more reflective and analytical part of the mind.

Give this puzzle a go to try some effortful, slow-brain, system-2 thinking. A bat and a ball together cost £1.10. The bat costs one pound more than the ball. How much is the ball? The intuitive answer is often 10 pence, but the correct answer is 5 pence for the ball and £1.05 for the bat!

Slow thinking involves focus, and sometimes critical reflection, whereby we slow down enough to consider our underlying beliefs. We think about where our thoughts came from and why. In doing so, we make more conscious, objective choices. This kind of analytical processing is helpful when weighing up intuitive decisions, where we can be inclined to make mistakes. Slow thinkers tend to be less impulsive (and may have difficulty with 'on-demand' responses).

In our fast-paced world of the internet and high-speed technology, slow thinking allows us to step back, breathe, regulate our emotions and then come to a point of view that is based on a more considered assessment of the information available.

In a nutshell
Requires attention and focus and delivers a thoughtful and accurate understanding of a situation.

Why it matters
Slow thinking can help people to improve their decision-making by minimizing entrenched cognitive biases.

Key figures
Niels Geiger
Daniel Kahneman, 1934–2024
Amos Tversky, 1937–1996

Make the connection

fast thinking

This is also known as automatic or intuitive thinking. Daniel Kahneman, in *Thinking Fast and Slow* (see opposite), describes it as system 1 thinking, in which no effort is required. It is automatic, frequent, emotional, stereotypic and unconscious. Examples of fast thinking range from reading a book or driving a car to holding cognitive and unconscious biases about people and situations. Kahneman gives lots of examples of fast thinking at play, like looking up when you hear a loud noise, or saying, 'Fine, thanks' when someone asks how you are. Working out 2x2 is fast thinking, unlike solving 28x31. Give it a try!

The main differences between fast and slow thinking are to do with effort and heuristics. (Heuristics are mental shortcuts or basic rules of thumb that help streamline decision making.) Fast thinking is often, but not always, emotionally driven and it is efficient; it is useful in situations that require a quick response, like an emergency, but is equally handy in making routine choices, like what to eat for breakfast. Fast thinking allows us to make decisions without extensive analysis, thus saving energy for more important tasks.

In his experiments, Kahneman concluded that fast thinking is associated with laziness, jumping to conclusions and a concept he termed WYSIWTI – 'what you see is what there is'. He also discusses the role of heuristics in fast thinking. The problem with these kinds of shortcuts, he says, is that they can lead to unconscious or even conscious biases and errors.

In a nutshell
Refers to the automatic, unconscious thinking that we engage in all the time.

Why it matters
Both fast and slow thinking styles are valuable and serve different purposes. Knowing when to employ each type of thinking is the key to successful decision-making.

Key figures
Daniel Kahneman, 1934–2024
Richard Threlkeld Cox, 1898–1991

Make the connection
change blindness, p.55
cognitive reappraisal, p.65
prejudice, p.138

memory

Memory is widely studied in psychology. It is a dynamic and complex cognitive function that involves the encoding, storage and retrieval of information. It shapes our identity, allows us to learn and helps us navigate the world in all its complexity.

Psychologists talk about memory as a 'system', with different elements. The first part of the memory system involves encoding. This is where we are able to transform sensory experiences into a form that can be stored in our brains. Once encoded, information can be stored for later use. Cognitive psychologists suggest that there are different types of storage – short- and long-term memory. The final stage of the system involves retrieval, where we bring stored memories back to consciousness for use in cognitive tasks.

With long-term memory comes episodic memory, the ability to recall specific events in our lives; semantic memory, which is tied to facts rather than events; and procedural memory, when we remember how to do specific tasks at an automatic level. like riding a bike.

Many factors affect the formation of memories. Adequate sleep, for example, is essential for consolidating memories and organizing information. Similarly, attention levels at times of encoding can also affect memory formation. Repetition and practice play important roles in moving memories from short- to long-term systems. Sometimes we remember through an association – a smell or a melody that brings memories back to awareness. It's complicated – you will definitely remember that!

In a nutshell
A complex cognitive process that involves coding, storage and retrieval of information.

Why it matters
A healthy operative memory underlies all aspects of our mental health and functional wellbeing. Without it we would literally be lost!

Key figures
Alan D. Castel
Elizabeth Loftus, b.1944
Daniel Shachter, b.1952

Make the connection
neuroplasticity, p.27
cognitive reserve, p.59
brain scans, p.150

forgetting

Forgetting, or disremembering, is the opposite to memory and is a natural and usual part of cognition. Forgetting is the apparent loss or modification of information already encoded and stored in our short- or long-term memories. Forgetting happens when we can't recall old memories. It can be gradual or spontaneous.

As with memory, there are many different theories of forgetting that have been explored in depth. In the 1880s, Hermann Ebbinghaus, a German psychologist, developed his forgetting curve after conducting word-retrieval experiments on himself. He concluded that much of what we forget is lost soon after it is originally learned. But he also said that the amount of forgetting levels off in time.

Around the same time, Sigmund Freud proposed that we forget things in order to push away bad thoughts and feelings. He called this process repression. Today we tend to divide this process into motivated forgetting, which is unconscious repression, and the more conscious thought suppression or avoidance.

Normal forgetting occurs all the time – we forget names, details of numbers or events that are not regularly practised. The most common cause of forgetting is to do with retaining new information as we age – this is known as decay theory. Amnesia is another type of forgetting, usually the result of brain injuries, neurological traumas or psychological traumas like abuse.

In a nutshell
The loss of information that had previously been stored in our short- or long-term memories. There are diverse theories as to why and how this occurs.

Why it matters
It is important to understand the process of forgetting to know what can help us in the future with remembering and learning.

Key figures
Charlotte Bühler, 1893–1974
Hermann Ebbinghaus, 1850–1909

Make the connection
dreaming, p.12
amnesia, p.98
cortex/limbic system, pp.144–5

brainwashing

Mind control and coercive persuasion are alternative names for what we commonly call 'brainwashing'. This is the systematic manipulation of beliefs, emotions, thoughts and behaviours to the point where the subject adopts those beliefs and behaviours. Brainwashing often involves a power differential and a coercive influence that works to control perceptions of reality.

The process of brainwashing gained notoriety in the Korean War of the 1950s. At that time reports emerged of USA prisoners of war making public confessions of their mistakes. They had apparently undergone a form of brainwashing.

The ultimate goal of brainwashing is to reprogram a person's beliefs and attitudes, replacing existing beliefs with a new ideological framework. There are several key elements that need to be present for brainwashing to occur – for example, isolation and manipulative techniques that break down resistence, like repetitive indoctrination, physical and emotional abuse. Cultic brainwashing practices involve charismatic leaders, group dynamics and rituals that reinforce a belief system. People in a cult are discouraged from dissenting and are subjected to constant reinforcement of the group's ideology. Information flow is controlled; there is fear and intimidation or social rejection if people do not conform to the dominant beliefs.

The notion of brainwashing has been sensationalized, but there is a widespread and understandable fascination with the question of whether or not our minds can be controlled.

In a nutshell
The process of pressurizing someone into adopting radically different beliefs.

Why it matters
To maintain a rational, critical society, it is useful to appreciate the mechanisms behind the systematic persuasion of non-believers.

Key figures
Steven Hassan, b.1954
Daniel Pick
Philip Zimbardo, b.1933

Make the connection
self-talk/ neurolinguistic programming, pp.34–5
fast thinking, p.39
left brain, right brain, p.148

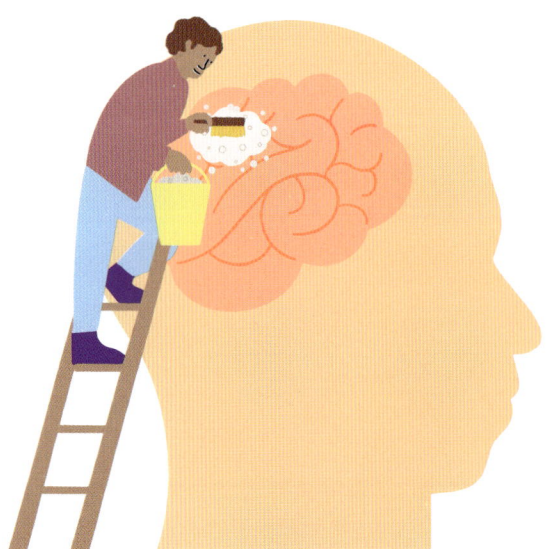

mind reading

The term 'mind reading' conjures up images of stage performers and fairground types looking deep into your soul and predicting your very next move. Some people associate mind reading with telepathy and use the words interchangeably. Telepathy really concerns the transfer of information from one person to another without use of the senses or direct contact; it is the remit of stage performers. The BBC, in 1927, conducted a telepathy experiment with radio listeners. They asked listeners to identify five different objects that the studio staff had selected, to see if the information could be transmitted over the airwaves. There was no evidence of telepathy, or mind reading, for that matter!

In psychological terms, mind reading describes perceptions and the ability to understand another person's feelings and experiences without actually being told them directly. How can this happen? Through noticing non-verbal cues, silences, how someone phrases something and the emotion that comes with a conversation. It is really to do with empathy and listening closely. The term 'mind reading' is often used metaphorically rather than literally.

Both mind reading and brainwashing concern the ability to know, or appear to know, another person's mental state. However, they are different in their meanings and applications. Whereas brainwashing has a manipulative, coercive aspect, mind reading is more of a natural process, which happens without pressure and is usually driven by a desire to empathize or connect with another person.

In a nutshell
The human ability to discern the thoughts of others without talking about it and especially by using extraordinary powers.

Why it matters
Mind reading, at the most basic level, can help us understand another's point of view and know when they are saying something that they do not entirely mean.

Key figures
Aaron Beck
Alain Morin
Frederic W.H. Myers

Make the connection
hypnosis, p.13
the unconscious, p.147
mind/brain, pp.154–5

intelligence

Human intelligence is, in essence, the capacity for thinking and understanding. It is thought to be made up of a combination of systems that enable us to perceive, process and respond to information. The term 'intelligence' came to be more widely used in the 1900s and most psychologists believe that it occurs in a number of domains: there is logical, musical, visuo-spatial, interpersonal and linguistic intelligence. These categories are often divided into three overarching areas: analytical, practical and creative intelligences. The terms 'book smart' and 'street smart' are useful in helping us to compare those who have an academic intelligence with those who can easily navigate the real world.

There is some debate about whether intelligence is genetically or environmentally formed and whether it can be neurologically explained. It is likely to be a combination.

English statistician Francis Galton (1822–1911) was the first to create a standardized test to measure intelligence. Later, Alfred Binet (1857–1911), a French psychologist, developed this idea, and now there are many tests that are standardized on different populations to assess different aspects of intelligence. The concept of an IQ or Intelligence Quotient score has been widely criticized for cultural and educational bias. David Wechsler, American psychologist and creator of the Wechsler Intelligence Scale, said that intelligence is 'a construct that implies an underlying reality, but this reality must be inferred from behavioural observations'.

In a nutshell
A concept created by humans that describes all aspects of human learning, adaptability and creativity.

Why it matters
It can be useful to know our intellectual strengths and weaknesses, so that we can maximize our potential in all areas of living and learning.

Key figures
Raymond Cattell, 1905–1998
Howard Gardner, b.1943
Edward Thorndike, 1874–1949

Make the connection
personality types/ the big five, pp.114–15
mind/brain, pp.154–5

wisdom

The difference between wisdom and intelligence concerns the application of knowledge. Wisdom is largely value orientated, and 'wise' decisions are often considered to be those based on the greater good. The question is not what you do or think, but 'Who or what does this serve?'

There is consensus that certain metacognitive processes – that is, thinking about thinking – are essential to wisdom. These processes are to do with reflection, self-awareness, seeing the bigger picture and integrating perspectives. Positive psychologists define wisdom as the coordination of knowledge and experience. Cognitive psychologists, meanwhile, surmise that wisdom must contain specific cognitive processes like intellectual humility or sensitivity.

Igor Grossman and his colleagues found in a 2017 study that regularly speaking in the third person increases the cognitive processes of wisdom – compromise, integration, sensitivity and perspective. They named this phenomenon Solomon's Paradox, suggesting that people reflect more wisely on the problems of others than on their own.

Wise people often have a more thoughtful and reflective approach to life and often see the bigger picture in, perhaps, a more detached and less emotional way. They tend to have more emotional balance or regulation, so that they don't get hooked into the smaller irritations or details of a complex situation.

In a nutshell
Wisdom is made up of a broad set of analytic, cognitive and emotional qualities that allow a holistic understanding of life.

Why it matters
Wisdom contributes to personal and societal wellbeing because it brings empathy, moral values and a reflective approach to our worldview.

Key figures
Susan Bluck
Judith Glück, b.1969
Igor Grossman

Make the connection
resilience, p.70
emotional intelligence/
theory of mind,
pp.136–7

false memories

Remember that holiday where you were sure you hung out on the beach all week (but in reality it was just one special day); or that time your little sister stole your favourite jumper (you actually loaned it to her)? These are all perfectly normal mishaps of memory, aka false memories. If you recall something that did not happen at all, or remember it differently from how it happened, this is a false memory.

One of the great contributors to false-memory theory is American psychologist Elizabeth Loftus. In the 1970s she demonstrated the influence of suggestibility on the creation of false memories, through experiments in which students were shown films of car accidents. When asked to estimate the speed of the cars from memory, students' answers varied widely depending on the phrasing of the question they were asked: did the cars 'collide' or 'smash each other'?

False memory occurs not just for individuals, but on a larger scale and in popular culture. Many people incorrectly recall lines from films or events in the world. Fiona Broome coined the term 'Mandela effect' after she discovered that she, along with others, believed that Nelson Mandela had died in the 1980s when in fact he died in 2013.

Psychological explanations for this phenomenon come from neuroscience and are concerned with the formation of schema, i.e., our organizational storage frameworks; confabulation, which involves the brain filling in missing gaps; misleading post-event information; and priming, or suggestibility, before event recall.

In a nutshell
Recollections of experiences and events that never happened. They are often detailed and vivid, and people who have them genuinely believe they are true.

Why it matters
How we see and recall events is important to us personally but also in the criminal courts.

Key figures
James Deese, 1921–1999
Pierre Janet, 1859–1947
Elizabeth Loftus, b.1944
Valerie F. Reyna, b.1955

Make the connection
psychopathy, p.123
prejudice/contact theory, pp.138–9

illusions

Illusions are perceptual experiences in which information from real, external stimuli creates false impressions of an item or event. In other words, the brain misinterprets a real stimulus (this is different from a hallucination, where there are no corresponding real-world stimuli). Illusions can take a variety of forms and occur through all the senses. They differ from false memories in that they happen 'here and now' and are not to do with recollection.

Many illusions occur in the same way across different people, a phenomenon which is thought to be due to commonalities in the visual processing mechanisms within our brains. The Müller-Lyer illusion is a good example: two identical lines look different in length depending on the way the arrow heads at each end are pointing.

Some people actually want to create their own illusions and use drugs to do so. LSD and cannabis contain psychometric agents that impair sensory perception and create what are mostly just illusions. These drugs are used recreationally, though scientists in the West are growing increasingly interested in the (controlled) use of substances like psilocybin, the hallucinogen in a magic mushroom, for relieving depression, trauma and other psychological distress.

In clinical settings, psychologists work with people who are experiencing visual illusions or hallucinations because they are suffering from the symptoms of schizophrenia. Psychiatrists can prescribe anti-psychotic medication to help alter their brain chemistry.

In a nutshell
Misperceptions of immediate sensory input. They are the discrepancy between sensory input and the interpretation of that input.

Why it matters
Our senses can deceive us. We need to be aware of this so as to be grounded in reality and free from making potentially dangerous mistakes.

Key figures
Hermann Ebbinghaus, 1850–1909
Ignaz Paul Vital Troxler, 1780–1866

Make the connection
dreaming/hypnosis, pp.12–13
psychedelic trips, p.97
schizophrenia, p.100

Rabbit or duck?

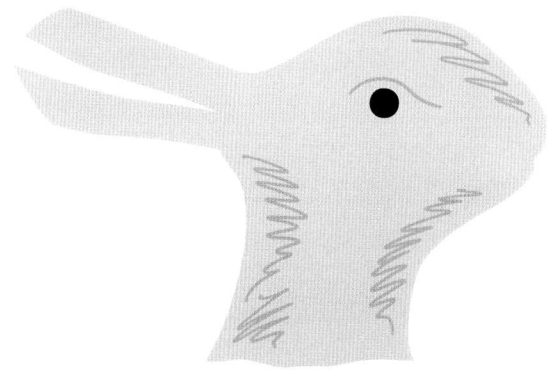

confirmation bias

A doctor sees a patient and makes a premature diagnosis; they seek out symptoms that confirm this diagnosis and ignore other information – this is an example of confirmation bias. The term refers to our tendency to favour information that supports our own beliefs and dismiss information that does not fit in with our world-view. It can deeply influence how we make decisions.

The term was coined by English psychologist Peter Wason (1924–2003) in the 1970s. He worked on the psychology of reasoning, trying to explain why people persistently commit logical errors. He said that cognitive bias occurs at different stages of information processing. For example, biased attention is when we selectively focus on information that confirms our point of view, whereas biased interpretation happens when we interpret information according to our beliefs, rather than the evidence in front of us. Biased memory, however, occurs when we selectively recall or discount memories.

Decision-making is influenced by confirmation bias, with potentially negative consequences. In legal settings confirmation bias can lead to injustices. Even our choices about health are impacted, so that we ignore evidence that does not go along with our own health beliefs.

We can try to overcome confirmation bias by raising our awareness and insight and by using critical thinking, examining various sources of information in reflective and objective ways. We should also be aware of the impact of social media on confirmation bias. Annoyingly, personalized algorithms show us images and messages we already favour.

In a nutshell
Our human tendency to favour information and experience that confirms our thinking about the world.

Why it matters
Acknowledging the existence of bias and understanding its impact on us can influence how we interpret information and make decisions for ourselves and in the world.

Key figures
Peter Cathcart Wason, 1924–2003
David Perkins
Scott Plous

Make the connection
fast thinking, p.39
shame, p.81
the unconscious, p.147

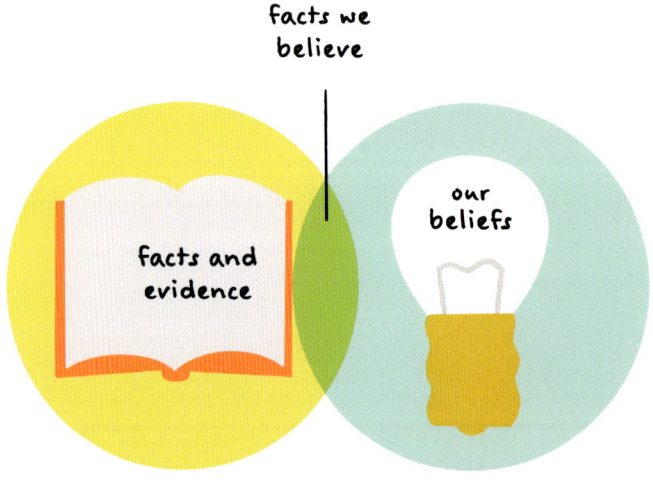

Facts we believe

our beliefs

facts and evidence

Dunning–Kruger effect

The human habit of thinking we are better at things than we actually are is referred to as the Dunning-Kruger effect, and it is a particular type of confirmation or cognitive bias. In 1999, social psychologists David Dunning and Justin Kruger carried out experiments looking at the relationship between a person's abilities and that same person's rating of their own abilities. Much as we like to think we know ourselves, it turns out that we are unable to accurately assess our own abilities.

It seems that contextual influences like gender, for example, play a part here. In one of the 1999 experiments, women and men performed equally well on a science quiz, but it may be no surprise to learn that women underestimated their performance, believing they had less scientific ability than their male counterparts.

It is thought that the effect may be due to a lack of metacognition – the ability to step back and look at things from the outside. Heuristics (mental shortcuts) are another explanation; in heuristic thinking we make incorrect decisions too quickly and have a tendency to see patterns where they don't exist, mistaking this for insight. Another cognitive mechanism may operate at those times when we have very little knowledge – i.e., we don't know what we don't know – and consequently we overestimate our capacities.

Everyone is susceptible to the Dunning-Kruger effect. Even the most expert scientist can assume knowledge and overestimate their own brilliance. Critical self-questioning, repeated practice and feedback from others are ways we can try to overcome this cognitive bias.

In a nutshell
A cognitive bias that refers to the overestimation of our own capabilities.

Why it matters
This effect highlights the importance of self-awareness, especially regarding gender and other biases, for rating performance.

Key figures
David Dunning, b.1960
Justin Kruger
Khalid Mahmood

Make the connection
decision-making, p.56
cognitive reappraisal, p.65
envy, p.82

But in my mind I'm 10/10.

5/10

mindfulness

Mindfulness involves being totally present in the moment – having a non-judgemental awareness of thoughts, feelings and sensations. It is, arguably, the Westernized version of meditation, which stems from ancient Buddhist traditions. The father of Western mindfulness, Jon Kabat-Zinn (b.1944), influenced by his road trips around India, introduced these Buddhist practices to Western medicine.

One of the aims of mindfulness practice is to reduce the chatter of inner dialogue and create deeper connections with life's current moments. Present-moment awareness, non-judgemental observation, focused attention, gratitude, acceptance and equanimity – a balanced, even way of being – are key concepts for mindful living. We can go some way to achieving these goals through mindful walking, breathing and the practice of body scanning.

Increasingly, research is being conducted in centres across the world to understand the relationship between mindfulness and wellbeing. In the UK there is the Oxford Mindfulness Research Centre and at Harvard, USA, there is the Thich Nhat Hanh Center for Mindfulness in Public Health, named after the Vietnamese Buddhist monk who also brought mindfulness to the attention of the West.

Research shows that mindfulness practice can improve mental and physical wellbeing, enhance cognitive function, and lead to better self-awareness and emotional regulation. Mindfulness doesn't have to be the sitting-on-a-mat kind of meditation: it can be introduced into daily activities like brushing your teeth!

In a nutshell
Deep presence and self-awareness. It is a centred, resilient and balanced approach to life.

Why it matters
As mindfulness practice and research grow across disciplines, they have the potential to promote mental health and foster a more conscious and compassionate society.

Key figures
Tara Brach, b.1953
Jon Kabat-Zinn, b.1944
Thich Nhat Hanh, 1926–2022

Make the connection
positive psychology, p.29
anxiety/depression, pp.88–9
the unconscious, p.147

mind wandering

Perhaps the direct opposite to mindfulness, mind wandering is not planned and not intentional. It diverts our attention from what we are doing right now, in this moment, to something completely unrelated. Mind wandering leads us from past memories to future planning, to grudges and obsessions. It is often conceived of as spontaneous thought – a kind of daydreaming. The best antidote to mind wandering? Mindfulness, of course!

Some neuroscientists think that mind wandering is connected to the default mode network (DMN), also known as the medial front-parietal network. This network of neurons is supposedly connected to self-referential thinking, introspection and mental exploration. There are objections to this view, though, and research into the neurological elements of mind wandering is ongoing.

Mind wandering can actually serve us well at times, helping with emotional regulation and providing us with space to process feelings. Some mind wandering can lead to those wonderful 'a-ha!' moments, like when you finally crack that crossword puzzle while doing something seemingly unrelated. Cognitive psychologists argue that mind wandering helps us with consolidating past memories and with future planning.

The downside is that drifting attention can create poor performance. It could lead to lapses in concentration and even accidents. Negative and excessive mind wandering can have a detrimental effect on emotional wellbeing, so it is important to stay aware of it.

In a nutshell

A spontaneous, unintentional shift of attention to self-generated images and thoughts, often unrelated to the present moment.

Why it matters

Mind wandering can give us an insight into our unacknowledged troubles and priorities, directing us to what needs further attention in our lives.

Key figures

Michael Kane
Rebecca McMillan
Jonathan
Smallwood, b.1975

Make the connection

synaesthesia

There are people for whom musical notes are a rainbow of colours, or for whom there is a cartoon-like connection between motion and sound, so that, for example, they hear a 'woosh!' when something goes past. These people have synaesthesia, and experience more than one sense simultaneously.

Synaesthesia occurs when the brain routes sensory information through multiple, unrelated senses. There are different types of synaesthesia. Perhaps the most well-known example is the above-mentioned sound–colour synaesthesia, where sound, music or sometimes speech is connected to colour hues. Someone with visual synaesthesia has a clear visual experience alongside hearing sounds. Mirror-touch synaesthesia is when someone sees something happen to someone else, but they actually feel it, too.

Why this happens is not fully understood. Neurologists suspect that it is something to do with atypical cross-activation between different regions of the brain, leading to a blending of sensory experiences. Using magnetic resonance imaging (fMRI) or magnetoencephalography (MEG), more areas of connectivity are being discovered.

Synaesthesia is probably hereditary and is usually discovered in childhood. Estimations of how common it is vary, but some studies suggest that 1 in 200 people may have the condition. For some it can be a wonderful experience - artists can incorporate their perceptions into their work. For others it can be overwhelming.

In a nutshell
A rare phenomenon, in which the interaction of neural connective pathways in the brain means that people perceive one sense through the pathway of a second.

Why it matters
The study of synaesthesia sheds light on sensory perception in all of us, showing the delicate interplay between the senses and how this creates diverse realities.

Key figures
Francis Galton, 1822–1911
Henry Paige

Make the connection
illusions, p.47
brain scans/electro-encephalography, pp.150–51

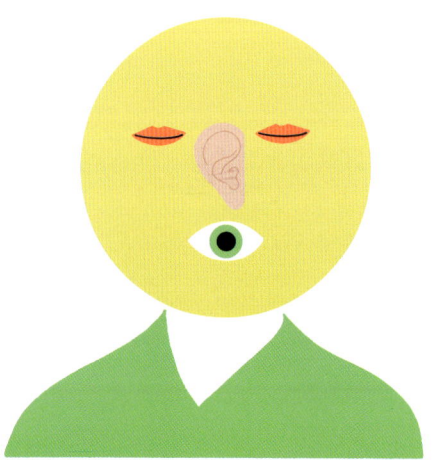

colour blindness

Although colour blindness is similar to synaesthesia, in that there is an issue with processing sensory information, the conditions are distinct. Sometimes called colour-vision deficiency, colour blindness causes a person to see colours differently from most other people; a person with colour blindess has difficulty telling colours apart. In colour blindness, there is difficulty with accurate perception; in synaesthesia the issue is to do with cross-modal perceptions that can't be controlled.

The most common form of colour blindness is that in which people can't distinguish between green and blue hues. But there are different colour blindnesses. Monochromacy is total colour blindness, where the world is seen in grayscale (it is extremely rare). Tritanopia, or blue-yellow colour blindness, is due to the malfunctioning or absence of cells that detect short wavelengths.

How do you know if you're colour blind? The Ishihara dot test is the most common method for diagnosing the condition. Named after its designer, Shinobu Ishihara, a professor at the University of Tokyo, the test is a series of plates with coloured dots. People have to decipher what number is showing among the dots.

Colour blindness is often inherited (mainly through the X chromosome), but can also be acquired through brain injury, age, illness or vitamin deficiency. It can impact in any setting where information is colour-coded.

In a nutshell
Colour–blind people can see colours differently from others; most of the time this colour deficiency makes it hard to see the difference between colours.

Why it matters
Where people are unable to see the full range of colours accurately it can lead to difficulties in educational settings as well as in day–to–day activities.

Key figures
John Dalton, 1766–1844
Shinobu Ishihara, 1879–1963
Semir Zeki, b.1940

Make the connection
dreaming/hypnosis, pp.12–13
cortex/limbic system, pp.144–5
left brain, right brain, p.148

attention

William James was the psychologist who, in 1890, first investigated the concept of human attention. He defined it as 'the taking possession by the mind, in clear and vivid form, of one out of what seem several simultaneously possible objects or trains of thought.' Our attention – our ability to actively process specific information from our environments while tuning out other details or irrelevant distractions – helps us make sense of the world around us.

Psychologists now know that the key facets of the concept are: sustained attention, also known as vigilance or concentration; divided attention, the ability to multitask; executive attention, involving the coordination of processes to manage conflicting information; and selective attention, or focusing on specific stimuli.

One classic example of the latter is what is known as the 'cocktail party effect': you are in the middle of a meaningful conversation with someone at a party and suddenly look away because you hear your name being said across the room. Psychologists suggest that the brain's sensory memory can segregate auditory stimuli subconsciously so that you are alerted to the sound of your name, even when focusing on something else.

Donald Broadbent's 'filter' model was a leading cognitive theory in this area, proposing that attention acts as a filter that allows only selected information to pass through conscious awareness. This links with Daniel Kahneman's more recent cognitive-bias theory that attentional resources are limited and must be allocated strategically.

In a nutshell
A dynamic cognitive process that shapes the perception of our world – we process specific information, while tuning out other details.

Why it matters
We need attention to be able to problem-solve, remember, communicate and fully carry out day-to-day tasks.

Key figures
Donald Broadbent, 1926–1993
William James, 1842–1910
Daniel Kahneman, 1934–2024

Make the connection
confirmation bias, p.48
cognitive reserve, p.59
anxiety, p.88

change blindness

People with change blindness fail to detect even pretty noticeable changes in visual scenes. There is a gap between what is actually changing and what is seen. Change blindness challenges the idea that we take a visual 'snapshot' of a scene all at once

George McConkie was one of the first scientists to come up with a study of change blindness in the 1970s. He measured participants' eye movements while words and texts were changed in front of them. When new words were added to a text, a significant number of participants failed to notice.

Change blindness is thought to be related to attentional theories, particularly in the area of attentional resources. The suggestion is that when attention is focused on one aspect of a text or visual scene, it is difficult to detect other changes at the same time.

Causes are put down to limited attentional capacity, where people cannot process a whole scene at once; visual saccades, where rapid eye movements suppress attention so that changes occurring at brief intervals may not be registered; and finally, cognitive inertia, where the mind resists recognizing deviations from what is expected in a scenario.

In a nutshell
Change blindness shows us that even though we may see events, we do not always fully perceive them.

Why it matters
Knowing about change blindness has implications for psychology and mental processing, as well as design and information delivery.

Key figures
George McConkie
Ronald Rensink
Alison Tollner–Burngasser

Make the connection
consciousness/ the unconscious, pp.146–7
brain scans/electro-encephalography, pp.150–51

decision-making

What was the last decision you made? What to have for breakfast? When to cross the road?

Decision-making is a cognitive reasoning process based on the beliefs and preferences of the decision-maker. Psychologists suggest that decision-making is highly context-dependent, with different responses elicited depending on the situation. You were going to choose just a cup of tea from the menu, but because your friend chose a whole breakfast fry-up you changed your mind. Our decisions are often tied up with those of other people. It all depends on context.

Conscious and unconscious cognitive bias also have key roles to play in how we make decisions. For example, we may well employ a job candidate who is just like us – unconscious bias in action.

Naturalistic decision-making research, which takes place in real-life environments, shows that in situations with less time, higher pressure or higher stakes (medical settings, for example), people use more fast thinking and intuitive decision-making. Although equally – in emergencies, for instance – analysis paralysis can occur: we are unable to make decisions because there is so much overwhelming information. Your child slips over and breaks his leg and you are paralysed and don't know what to do. This is partly why hospitals, airlines and the like have emergency protocols. We can get stuck, going over information time and again for fear of making the wrong decision, and protocols can get us out of this loop.

In a nutshell
A complicated aspect of human cognition. Psychologists from neurological, social and cognitive branches study this phenomenon.

Why it matters
Understanding how decisions are made and knowing the challenges to effective decision-making can make for smoother, safer societies.

Key figures
Erich Brockmann
Antonio Damasio, b.1944
Herbert A. Simon, 1916–2001

Make the connection
fast thinking, p.39
confirmation bias, p.48
moods, p.66

procrastination

This is the opposite end of the spectrum to decision-making and not limited to humans. Experiments have shown that pigeons will choose a delayed complex task over an easy immediate one. Everyone likes to procrastinate! Many of us will be familiar with procrastination and its negative consequences: increased stress, reduced productivity and missed opportunities.

Why do we procrastinate when we know it is not good for us? Perfectionism might be part of the answer and it often goes hand-in-hand with procrastination. Longing to achieve the perfect grade, we delay writing the assignment to avoid disappointment if we don't get it. Procrastination can, however, be culture-dependent. According to a 2023 study by Shazia Rehman, in Western cultures students tend to procrastinate in order to avoid doing worse than they have done before, whereas students from non-Western cultures tend to procrastinate to avoid looking stupid in front of their peers.

When faced with a difficult task, reframing and self-talk can help spur us into action. Don't like cleaning the kitchen? 'It will be so fresh when I am done, some vigorous cleaning makes for good exercise. I can listen to some music while I do it!' Reframing is an antidote to procrastination, as is a little bit of critical self-reflection – investigating what exactly it is that we are avoiding and naming it can really help shift us into action!

In a nutshell
The intentional delay or postponement of tasks, leading to a gap between intention and action. It can lead to stress, low self–esteem and frustration.

Why it matters
Examining why we are procrastinating can lead us to explore ideas about success, failure, confidence and sadness; it can help us move on and grow.

Key figures
Roy Baumeister, b.1953
Timothy A. Pychyl
Dianne Tice

Make the connection
attention/change blindness, pp.54–5
stress/burnout, pp.76–7
perfectionism, p.91

bilingualism

People who are bilingual use two languages interchangeably – they can speak, understand, read and write proficiently in both.

Simultaneous bilingualism occurs in babies and toddlers who are exposed to two languages at a very early age, usually below three years. This tends to happen in multilingual households where parents or grandparents come from different countries. There is no truth in the myth that young children can be confused by having two languages spoken at home, although it is true to say bilingual children may start speaking a little later than their peers.

Sequential bilingualism happens after a child has developed a first language. It usually evolves through life experiences, like moving countries, and through formal or informal education.

From a psychological perspective it is interesting to investigate the neurological and cognitive mechanisms of bilingualism. Social and clinical psychologists explore the complexities of how people with two languages identify with both cultures, how this varies in different contexts and also how they are perceived by others.

Research has shown that there are cognitive benefits to bilingualism. Bilingual students may have advantages in cognitive flexibility, problem-solving and metalinguistic awareness, i.e. the ability to reflect on the structure and conventions of language. Consequently, in some schools – in Wales or Ireland, for example – bilingualism is written into policies at institutional and national levels.

In a nutshell
Proficiency in two languages. This can come at an early age or can be acquired later.

Why it matters
Understanding the mechanisms of bilingualism adds to our appreciation of linguistic diversity and can help institutions to support diverse groups and societies.

Key figures
Jim Cummins, b.1949
Wallace Lambert, 1922–2009
Elizabeth Peal

Make the connection
neuroplasticity, p.27
dyslexia, p.61
twins, p.118

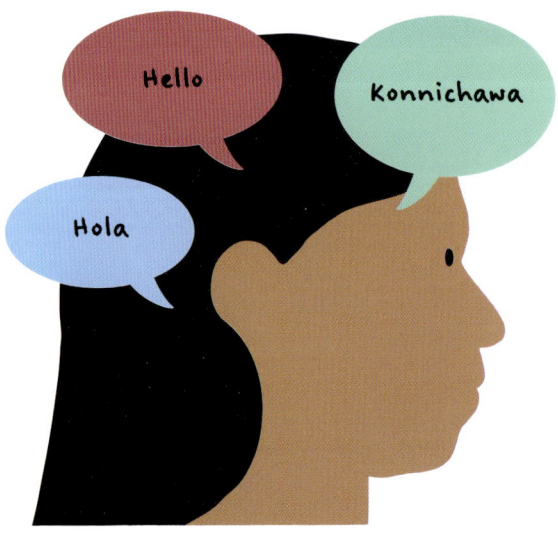

cognitive reserve

This is the term used to describe the mind's ability to endure age-related changes and neurological damage while still maintaining cognitive function. The concept originated in the late 1980s, when researchers described individuals with no apparent symptoms of dementia who, at autopsy, were found to have brain changes in line with advanced Alzheimer's disease. These people did not show symptoms of the disease when alive because they had enough 'cognitive reserve' to offset the damage and continue as usual.

More recent research has shown that people with greater cognitive reserve are better able to stave off the degenerative brain changes associated with dementia, Parkinson's disease, stroke or other diseases. Lifestyle greatly impacts on the development and maintenance of cognitive reserve: eating a plant-based diet, regular exercise, getting enough sleep, managing stress, nurturing social contacts and continuing to challenge your brain in different ways. Learning a new language certainly belongs on this list – in this respect, bilingualism is connected to cognitive reserve.

The cognitive-reserve hypothesis proposes that those of us with bigger brains and greater neural density may have more cognitive reserve. A larger brain can provide more neural resources and this compensates for deficits in other areas. People with a greater level of cognitive reserve show more efficient cognitive processing, allowing the brain to compensate for age-related change or neurological damage by using alternative neural networks.

In a nutshell
Describes the brain's resilient and adaptable capacity to maintain cognitive function in the face of aging and neurological damage or disease.

Why it matters
Research in this area has implications for understanding individual differences in aging and interventions that foster cognitive good health as we grow older.

Key figures
Daniel Barulli
Yaakov Stern

Make the connection
neurolinguistic programming, p.35
Alzheimer's/ Parkinson's disease, pp.152–3

aphasia

Aphasia, sometimes called dysphasia, is a language disorder that affects how we communicate, speak, understand, read and write. It is usually caused by damage to the language centres of the brain.

Aphasia can manifest in lots of different ways, depending on where the brain damage is, and the extent of that damage. Causes of brain-damage aphasia include stroke, sudden brain injury due to impact or infection, tumours or neurodegenerative diseases like Alzheimer's.

There are several different types of aphasia, with different names, and located in different parts of the brain. People with Broca's aphasias – usually caused by damage to Broca's area of the brain, in the left frontal lobe – often produce short sentences, with relatively little perceived comprehension. Wernicke's aphasia primarily impacts on language comprehension; sufferers create fluent but nonsensical speech and have an impaired understanding of written language. They often create neologisms – newly made-up words. Anomic aphasias are marked by word-finding difficulties.

Speech and language therapy and cognitive rehabilitation that focuses on memory games and overall cognitive functioning are the main treatments for aphasia. Talking therapies and supportive group and family therapy are also helpful. Some people improve a great deal with these kinds of interventions, but others shift very little. Improvement is usually connected to the severity and location of the injury as well as individual differences.

In a nutshell
A complex language disorder caused by damage to the language centres of the brain. This impacts on all areas of communication.

Why it matters
Psychologists and others can offer useful interventions for those who suffer with aphasia. Research is vital to creating rehabilitation treatments in this area.

Key figures
Paul Broca, 1824–1880
Armand Trousseau, 1801–1867
Carl Wernicke, 1848–1905

Make the connection
left brain, right brain/ lateralization, p.149
mind/brain, pp.154–5

dyslexia

This neurological condition is believed to affect nearly 10 per cent of the population, impacting the ability to read, write and spell. As in aphasia, the way the brain is processing information is not fully functioning. This is not due to damage, however – the exact causes of dyslexia are unknown, but it is thought that genetics plays a large role in the brain development of people who have it.

People with dyslexia have difficulty decoding, recognizing and spelling words. This was mislabelled as stupidity or low ability until quite recently, with consequences for the self-esteem of people with the condition. Things have, thankfully, changed, and dyslexia is recognized in the classroom, the work place and at universities.

People with dyslexia have difficulties with phoneme awareness and the ability to identify individual sounds within words. They struggle with converting the written word into speech and have reading fluency issues. They are often much slower readers than non-dyslexics. Difficulties in applying spelling rules, struggles with letter reversals like b and d, alongside limitations in working memory make for more challenging academic lives for those with dyslexia. Teachers and others can help with designing useful interventions to address the unique learning needs of each dyslexic.

There is a surge in advocacy and awareness groups for dyslexia, with famous faces – Keira Knightley and Richard Branson are high-profile dyslexics – trying to promote understanding and dispel myths.

In a nutshell
A specific learning difficulty that affects skills involved in accurate and fluent reading and spelling.

Why it matters
If we can identify dyslexic tendencies early and intervene with supportive strategies, then people can reach their true potential and have higher self-esteem as a result.

Key figures
Oswald Berkhan, 1834–1917
Rudolf Berlin, 1833–1897

Make the connection
memory/forgetting, pp.40–41
attention, p.54
bilingualism, p.58

flashbacks

Flashbacks are vivid experiences in which we relive aspects of a traumatic event or feel as if it is happening right now. In somatic flashbacks, the mind and body react accordingly, creating the very same sensations in the nervous system and making the sufferer feel like they are back at the original event: breathless, with rapid heartbeat, sweating, fear, panic and so on.

Very little experimental research on flashbacks has been conducted because experts have felt that these fragile, involuntary memory experiences would be too uncomfortable and too unethical to study. There has, however, been research into flashbacks as they occur in the real world, using people who have suffered the traumas of abuse, violence or war. Flashbacks are nearly always connected to symptoms of post-traumatic stress disorder (PTSD) or cPTSD (the 'c' stands for 'complex'). PTSD occurs as a consequence of traumas including sexual assault, bullying and even childbirth.

People who have flashbacks sometimes describe the experience as being like a video of events replaying in their mind. Flashbacks can be triggered by a cue or a reminder linked to the actual external experience, like a loud banging noise for a war veteran.

Theories of the function and purpose of flashbacks vary, but many psychologists believe that they serve as a coping mechanism, helping trauma survivors to make sense of their experiences. By reliving the traumatic events through flashbacks, it is thought that we can come to terms with and gain control over what has happened to us.

In a nutshell
Memories that appear in the consciousness of a person, even when they don't plan it or don't want to remember. They are mainly associated with PTSD.

Why it matters
To help with people suffering from post-traumatic stress and alleviate their distress, we need to understand the workings of flashbacks.

Key figures
Alan Baddeley, b.1934
Chris Brewin, b.1953
Hermann Ebbinghaus, 1850–1909

Make the connection
illusions, p.47
mind wandering, p.51
psychedelic trips, p.97

hallucinations

While both hallucinations and flashbacks involve altered perceptions, the main difference concerns the sources of perception. Hallucinations are to do with perceptions that are not real and never were. In contrast, flashbacks are to do with re-experiencing past events that were very real. Hallucinations can be very distressing for the person experiencing them. They can be perceived through any of the five senses and are usually associated with medical and psychiatric conditions like schizophrenia and bipolar disorder.

The emotional content of schizophrenic hallucinations can be disturbing, and often manifests as a voice cursing the subject. 55 per cent of auditory hallucinations for schizophrenics are malicious in content. Some people who hear voices manage these auditory hallucinations; others actually befriend them. Visual hallucinations are also often present in those with schizophrenia. These can be visual illusions or distortions of real external stimuli.

Hallucinations like hearing voices are not experienced only by those with schizophrenia. In a small 2015 survey, people with a wide range of psychiatric diagnoses were found to be hearing voices. These psychiatric conditions included bipolar disorder, depression and generalized anxiety disorder. Oliver Sacks, the well-known British neurologist, described his own auditory hallucinations.

People with no psychiatric disorder can also experience hallucinations when they take mind-altering substances like cannabis, cocaine and amphetamines.

In a nutshell
False perceptions that are not present in our external environments.

Why it matters
Studying hallucinations, whether drug–induced, trauma–related or otherwise, is essential for understanding the working mind and offering appropriate therapeutic interventions.

Key figures
Richard Bentall, b.1956
David Rosenhan, 1929–2012

Make the connection
moods, p.66
psychedelic trips, p.97
the unconscious, p.147

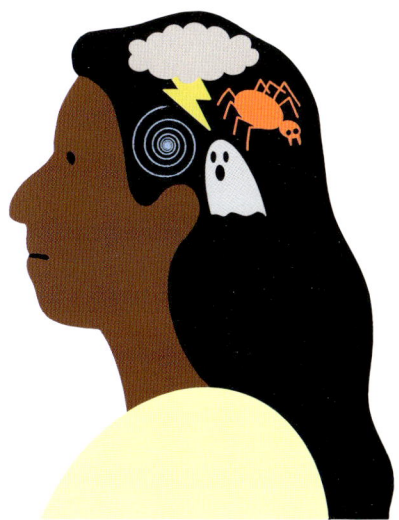

cognitive dissonance

We know that smoking damages our health, yet we still smoke. This creates a feeling of discomfort inside us so that something has to change: we might give up smoking so that our values and behaviours are aligned. Or we might instead downplay the health risks associated with smoking...

Cognitive dissonance is a psychological phenomenon that happens when we hold two contradictory beliefs at the same time. It is the feeling of discomfort that we have when our behaviours do not align with our values and beliefs. This discomfort, more often than not, will drive us to reduce the inconsistency and try to restore a sense of internal harmony. We can do this by temporarily changing either our beliefs or our behaviours.

American cognitive psychologist Leo Festinger introduced the theory in 1957. He proposed that humans strive for psychological consistency in order to function with ease in the world. Coping with paradoxical or contradictory ideas is stressful and takes a lot of energy, so we change in some way to make life easier for ourselves.

This concept is useful in therapy and can be used to develop interventions to help facilitate change. Similarly, in educational settings it is helpful to use cognitive dissonance to induce learning and even raise awareness about values and behaviours.

In a nutshell
The discomfort that people experience when their beliefs and values do not match their behaviours.

Why it matters
Understanding this phenomenon provides policymakers, teachers and others with subtle ways into behaviour change and the way people manage inconsistencies.

Key figures
Merrill Carlsmith, 1936–1984
Joel Cooper
Leo Festinger, 1919–1989

Make the connection
anxiety, p.88
motivational interviewing, p.108
conformity, p.131

cognitive reappraisal

Cognitive reappraisal, like cognitive dissonance, concerns thinking and behaviour, but cognitive reappraisal has a very different flavour. It is an emotional-regulation strategy that involves changing the way we think about a situation in response to our bodily experience. Rather than immersing ourselves in angry thoughts and feelings about a situation, for example, cognitive reappraisal means that we take a step back and try to view the provocative event in a calmer, more objective way. By reinterpreting, reanalysing or reframing a situation, we can alter our emotional reactions to it and create a more adaptive and helpful response to the external stressors. Easier said than done!

American psychologists Richard Lazarus and Susan Folkman developed this theory. In primary cognitive appraisal, they say, a person decides if an event is dangerous or stressful; in secondary appraisal they decide whether they are able to cope with this specific stress. So, you might have a work deadline that you are worrying about. You might cognitively reappraise this as a chance to complete the work, show off your abilities and enhance your own personal growth. Similarly, when dealing with an unexpected change, you can either decide that this is terrible news and panic or you can reappraise and realize there are lots of opportunities in such a change.

Doing this effectively requires practice and the right context – it is not going to work in every situation and nor should it.

In a nutshell

A cognitive emotion-regulation strategy that involves consciously changing the way we interpret a situation to help reshape our responses.

Why it matters

This is an adaptive approach that can reduce stress, balance our emotions and contribute to overall mental health.

Key figures

Susan Folkman, b.1938
Richard Lazarus, 1922–2002

Make the connection

memory/forgetting, pp.40–41
mind reading, p.43
anxiety, p.88

moods

A mood is an affective state that is often categorized as positive or negative. All kinds of factors – environmental, physical and even historical – can affect our moods, from winning the lottery to noisy neighbours. Physiological influences like nutrition, hormones and general fitness can also have an impact.

Moods are regulated by neurotransmitters like serotonin, dopamine and norepinephrine – chemical substances released by the nerve fibres in our brains. Psychiatric medication corrects imbalances in these chemicals. Psychologists, by contrast, work with moods by looking at our thinking patterns. Cognitions, or interpretations of events, shape the way we are feeling. If you believe that someone ignored you at a party, for example, it might bring down your mood, making you feel sad and small. In fact that person may just be short-sighted or may not have recognized you; knowing this would have changed your cognitions from sad to compassionate, perhaps. Psychoanalysis would probably explain moods in terms of the unconscious or early childhood experiences: moods are dependent on projections and transferences that evolve from younger years, according to psychoanalysts.

Life events and the contexts we live in also impact on mood, with Albert Bandura's social-learning theory suggesting that mood is kind of contagious – we learn it from those around us, emulating moods that seem to elicit social 'reward'.

In a nutshell
A mood is a general feeling we have, rather than a reaction to a specific situation.

Why it matters
How we function in the world is dependent on how we feel inside. Understanding what contributes to good or bad moods can help us to live more enjoyable lives.

Key figures
Richard Davidson, b.1951
Lisa Feldman Barrett, b.1963
Joseph E. LeDoux, b.1949

Make the connection
psychiatric medicine, p.103
personality types, p.114
emotional intelligence, p.136

emotions

The terms mood and emotion are both wrapped up with how we feel. Emotions are short-lived, while moods tend to last longer and have no specific starting point or trigger.

Much of psychology centres on understanding the nature, development and maintenance of emotional experiences. One of the best-known theories in experimental psychology is the James-Lange theory of emotions, which proposes that emotions arise from physiological responses to stimuli. We notice changes in our bodies that are triggered by external events, which then lead to emotional experiences. As always with psychology, there is disagreement in the research field! The Cannon-Bard theory suggests that physiological arousal and emotional experiences occur *simultaneously* in response to stimuli, rather than one causing the other. Hearing a loud bang outside leads to a racing heart and faster breathing and we feel scared – our emotion is fear. It is hard to disentangle whether this process is sequential or simultaneous.

Outside of experimental laboratories, psychological therapy plays an important role in helping people cope with emotions. Therapeutic focus is on emotional regulation or the ability to manage our own emotions. Emotional focused therapy (EFT) and dialectical behavioural therapy (DBT) specifically focus on managing emotions through mindfulness; distress tolerance, i.e. managing actual or perceived emotional distress; and interpersonal effectiveness training, i.e. getting on with others while managing yourself.

In a nutshell
Reactions to specific events or triggers that impact on the way we feel physically and mentally.

Why it matters
How we feel influences all aspects of our waking lives. Understanding how it all works can facilitate balanced living.

Key figures
Daniel Batson, b.1943
Robert Cialdini, b.1945
Paul Ekman, b.1934

Make the connection
neuroticism, p.71
grief, p.74
guilt/shame, pp.80–81

mental health

Mental health is a state of wellbeing that allows us to cope with the stresses of daily life. This includes our emotional, physical, psychological and social wellbeing.

In 1946, the World Health Organization (WHO) stated that mental wellbeing is an important part of overall health. Mental health emerged as its own field of study, having not been acknowledged previously. According to WHO statistics, over 700,000 people take their own lives each year – about one person every 40 seconds. According to the British National Health Service (NHS), one in five people have suicidal thoughts and one in fourteen self-harm. Understanding the complexities of mental health is therefore crucial.

Stigma around mental health exists, but less so than in past eras. Since the global pandemic and with exposure to social media, many more people have realized the value of good mental health and the importance of treatment if it is required, even without a mental illness diagnosis.

Psychological theories addressing mental health are numerous. Perhaps the neatest and most influential one is the biopsychosocial model. In 1977 a medic, George Engel, coined the term biopsychosocial for understanding ill health. As the name suggests, the approach emphasizes understanding health and mental health in context, considering the interaction between biological, psychological and social factors in mental health and wellbeing.

In a nutshell
Refers to emotional wellbeing and how we cope with the stresses, the ups and downs, of daily life.

Why it matters
Good mental health allows us to fulfil our potential, be productive and play an active role in our communities.

Key figures
George L. Engel, 1913–1999
David Harper & Paula Reavey
Mark Williamson

Make the connection
resilience, p.70
flow states, p.96

mental illness

The polar opposite of mental health, mental illness negatively affects one's ability to function in the world. It is characterized by a clinically significant disturbance in cognitions, behaviour and emotional regulation.

There are many kinds of mental illness, including mood disorders, anxiety, eating disorders, psychosis and schizophrenia. People with mental illness regularly feel distressed and out of control of their lives. Mental illnesses are usually diagnosed when we, or our loved ones, realize that we are no longer coping with day-to-day life. A medical practitioner diagnoses a mental illness by carrying out an assessment and taking a detailed history. Sometimes they will use checklists and questionnaires. There is no blood test, no brain scan, for mental illness – it is all based on the self-reporting of the sufferer.

Medical professionals base their diagnoses on the DSM – *The Diagnostic and Statistical Mannual of Mental Disorders*. This is now in its fifth version (DSM-5-TR was published in 2022 by the American Psychiatric Association). There is great deal of controversy about the reliability and validity of the DSM, as well as its implicit individualizing of societal distress. However, many people experience relief and gratitude after receiving a diagnosis and associated treatments for their disturbing experiences.

In a nutshell
Mental illnesses are serious mental, behavioural or emotional disorders.

Why it matters
Understanding and successfully treating mental illness can help families, communities and societies.

Key figures
Mary Boyle
James Davies
R. D. Laing

Make the connection
counsellor/clinical psychologist, pp.8–9
borderline personality disorder/bipolar disorder, pp.94–5
schizophrenia/ psychosis, pp.100–101
psychotherapy/ psychiatric medication, pp.102–103

resilience

Nylon is a material that always bounces back into shape – it is resilient! Psychological resilience happens when people face their difficulties and adapt to them, instead of falling into despair or using unhealthy coping strategies. Rather than mental toughness, psychologists prefer to think of it as 'bounce-backability' – the capacity to withstand or recover quickly from difficulties.

In the late 1970s, psychology researchers felt that too much emphasis had gone into studying vulnerability and risk factors. They turned the research on its head and started to investigate what makes people cope, rather than what makes them crumble in adversity. This represented the start of a shift from 'deficit-focused' to 'strengths-focused' approaches to understanding human behaviours.

Psychologists suggest numerous causes for resilience: they put it down to both internal and external characteristics, including mental health, physical fitness, genetics, environment and social support. Resilient people also tend to possess characteristics like good communication skills, an internal locus of control (they believe they have control over their own lives), high emotional intelligence, positive views of themselves and their abilities. They see themselves as fighters, survivors or 'powerpeople'.

On top of these individual characteristics, social support is a highly significant and often underestimated contributor to human resilience. 'No man is an island,' said the poet John Donne. We need our communities to help us in challenging times.

In a nutshell
The psychological strength to cope with stress at times of hardship. A number of internal and external factors combine to create resilience.

Why it matters
Challenges are inevitably a part of life's journey; we need to know what helps and hinders us when faced with setbacks.

Key figures
Carol Dweck, b.1946
Norman Garmezy, 1918–2009
Emmy Werner, 1929–2017

Make the connection
positive psychology, p.29
traits/social roles, pp.112–13
self–esteem/self–efficacy, pp.126–7

When life gives you lemons, make lemonade.

neuroticism

The characteristics of neuroticism are almost the polar opposite of those of resilience. For the neurotic person the glass is usually half empty. The resilient will work out how to fill the glass to the best level possible. Some common traits of neuroticism are feelings of anxiety, irritability, self-doubt and viewing minor problems as overwhelming. It exists on a continuum – we can have high, middling or low levels of neuroticism.

For Sigmund Freud, who introduced neuroticism into mainstream culture, it could be explained as a psychic conflict between two opposing unconscious forces. Freud said that neuroticism is the result of a conflict between superego and ego, with the former oppressing the reasonably healthy person and causing them to behave in neurotic ways. Hans Eysenck, a German-born British psychologist, later expanded on these ideas. Eysenck's 'big three' model defines three core personality traits: extroversion, neuroticism and psychoticism. Neurotic personalities are innate and genetically based in Eysenck's model. Robert R. McCrae and Paul Costa, in the early 2000s, described our personalities as having five essential factors (the five factors model, or FFM). Neuroticism is one of the key dimensions, along with openness to experience, conscientiousness, extroversion and agreeableness.

Such traits are usually measured by self-report questionnaires as part of a personality assessment.

In a nutshell
A personality trait characterized by a tendency towards anxiety, instability and negative emotions.

Why it matters
Through understanding a person's level of neuroticism, psychologists can create and tailor interventions for the workplace or the therapy space.

Key figures
Hans Eysenck, 1916–1997
Sigmund Freud, 1856–1939
Karen Horney, 1885–1952

Make the connection
psychotherapy, p.102
traits, p.112
personality types/the big five, pp.114–15

happiness

According to researcher Sonja Lyubomirsky, happiness is 'the experience of joy, contentment or positive wellbeing, combined with a sense that one's life is good, meaningful and worthwhile.'

How happiness actually looks varies immensely: your idea of happiness might be sleeping out under the stars, but your best friend gets total joy from staying out all night clubbing. Because of these discrepancies, social scientists tend to use the term 'subjective wellbeing' in their studies of happiness. The two key elements of subjective wellbeing are: the balance of emotions – for happiness this means more positive than negative ones; and life satisfaction – how content or satisfied you are with different areas of your life, like relationships, work and any other areas that you consider important.

While perceptions of happiness and what makes us happy are different in everyone, signs of happiness are universal. These include feeling like you have the life you wanted, that your conditions in life are good, that you have accomplished or will accomplish all that you want in life, experiencing gratitude and wanting to share your happiness with others.

One influential psychological framework for understanding happiness is called the hedonic framework. This emphasizes the pursuit of good feelings and the avoidance of pain as central to happiness. Conversely, the eudaimonic perspective focuses on self-realization, personal growth and the pursuit of meaningful goals.

In a nutshell
An emotional state characterized by joy, satisfaction and a sense of wellbeing.

Why it matters
Positive emotions, like happiness, are good for us. Happiness reduces stress hormones, eases feelings of anxiety and depression and improves our immune systems.

Key figures
Mihalyi Csikszentmihalyi, 1934–2021
Erich Fromm, 1900–1980
Martin Seligman, b.1942

Make the connection
positive psychology, p.29
resilience, p.70
empathy, p.140

hedonism

The difference between hedonism and happiness is that happiness (sometimes called 'eudaimonic happiness') is achieved through experiences of meaning, purpose, virtue and growth. Hedonism, on the other hand, also known as 'hedonic happiness', is achieved through the pursuit of pleasure and enjoyment only – without the meaning, growth and virtue bit! The term is used in philosophy and art as well as in psychology, and includes sensory pleasure in addition to more intellectual pleasures.

Evolutionary psychology provides useful insights into the adaptive function of hedonistic behaviours, theorizing that the urge to seek pleasure and avoid pain has evolved as a fundamental strategy for survival and reproduction. Our hedonistic tendencies may have provided our ancestors with evolutionary advantage, enhancing the chances of survival and reproductive success.

Psychological or motivational theories of hedonism state that human behaviour is determined by the desire to increase pleasure and minimize pain. This process is often linked to egoism in psychology, where each person aspires only to their *own* individual happiness. Thomas Hobbes, the seventeenth-century English philosopher and author of *Leviathan*, argued that our egos are the primary impulse in determining all our behaviours – this would include hedonism!

Other branches of psychology, like cognitive and psychoanalytical, work with hedonistic people to engage their beliefs, pleasure-seeking and pain-avoidance behaviours.

In a nutshell
Hedonism theorizes that all pleasure is intrinsically valuable and all pain is not. In hedonism no attention is paid to meaning, values and growth.

Why it matters
Hedonism is that wonderful feeling of pleasure with no consideration of consequences. It can bring social problems, however, if it is not kept in check.

Key figures
Jeremy Bentham, 1748–1832
Shane J. Lopez, 1970–2016
John Stuart Mill, 1808–1873

Make the connection
ego, p.11
growth mindset/sports psychology, pp.32–3

grief

Grief is a normal response to a major loss, be that the death of a loved one, miscarriage, or other life losses like redundancy, moving house or a change in health status. There are many psychological theories that try to understand the grieving process. The most well-known is the five stages of grief model, developed in the 1960s by Elisabeth Kübler-Ross, a Swiss–American psychiatrist. Her theory has been criticized for its simplicity, but it is still very much in use and is sometimes valuable. The five Kübler-Ross stages are: denial, anger, bargaining, depression and acceptance. Grieving people move through these sequential steps, according to her theory.

A more recent, increasingly popular grief theory, sometimes called the fried-egg theory, was developed by Lois Tonkin in 1996. She called this 'growing around grief'. Imagine drawing a circle to represent your life. Shade in the circle to represent grief. At the start of a bereavement, or any other loss, the whole circle will be shaded – it will all be the yellow of the fried egg – but over the years the size of the yellow shading shrinks, and there is more 'egg white' as the rest of your world expands.

Another useful concept to explain grief is attachment theory, which highlights the enduring bonds and profound impact of attachment on the grieving process.

Continuing-bonds theory suggests that people keep up a connection with the deceased, or lost thing, through ongoing memories, rituals and relationships. This theory challenges the notion that successful grieving involves complete detachment from the deceased. There is comfort in maintaining some connection with them.

In a nutshell
The strong, sometimes overwhelming, feelings we experience when there is loss.

Why it matters
The experience of loss affects all of us during the course of a lifetime. Psychological theories of grief can facilitate healing and make mourners feel less isolated.

Key figures
Sigmund Freud, 1856–1939
Elisabeth Kübler-Ross, 1926–2004
Lois Tonkin

Make the connection
melancholia/languishing, pp.78–9
anxiety/depression, pp.88–9
bonding/anxious attachment, pp.124–5

separation

In 1969, John Bowlby, British psychiatrist and psychoanalyst, wrote a paper called 'Attachment and Loss', in which he explained his understanding of the separation process in infants and their carers. According to his theory, we form strong emotional bonds with primary caregivers early in life. This is the 'secure base' from which we can explore the world. Separation from these close attachment figures can lead to anxiety and distress, making us want to get closer to them, seeking security or comfort. Bowlby suggested that four different attachment styles exist in children: secure, anxious, avoidant and fearful, each affecting the ease of separation. The theory has been criticized by those who argue that children can form more than one bond, and for its overemphasis on 'mother' rather than 'carer' – remember it was published in the 1950s!

Separation is, then, the other side of the coin to attachment and, in psychological terms, refers to the loss or absence of significant attachment figures. It is related to loss and grieving, but is a less temporally and emotionally distinct process.

Ecological systems theory, the work of Urie Bronfenbrenner in the 1970s, focuses on the role of the environmental context in shaping individual experiences of separation. Separation happens within layers of environmental systems: family, school, community and culture. These contexts all influence the norms of separation and how it affects identity and belonging.

In a nutshell
In psychology, the loss or absence of significant attachment figures, relationships or environments.

Why it matters
Separation can prevent people from living rich, full lives. Understanding how separation works can help to alleviate the anxiety and upset it causes.

Key figures
John Bowlby, 1907–1990
Urie Bronfenbrenner, 1917–2005
Donald Winnicott, 1896–1971

Make the connection
memory/forgetting, pp.40–41
cognitive dissonance, p.64
love, p.128

stress

Stress is a set of physiological and psychological responses to demands that exceed our coping abilities. It manifests in emotional, physical and cognitive disturbances.

Signs of stress play out in four main domains: psychological – anxiety, worrying, difficulty concentrating; physical – high blood pressure, weight change or low immunity; emotional – irritability, feelings of overwhelm, excessive crying; and behavioural – poor self-care, addictions, and so on.

There are many causes of stress, but they include relationships, finances, health and work challenges. Difficult events trigger the body's fight or flight responses. Hormones like cortisol and adrenaline are released in response to the perceived threat. When the threat goes, systems should return to normal, but with chronic stress this does not happen, and this can result in bodily damage.

For clinical and other practising psychologists, the biopsychosocial model is a valuable way to explain stress, with its focus on genetic factors, internal psyche and wider social environments as contributing factors. Practitioners also use the 'stress bucket' metaphor: our stress buckets might be different sizes, but whatever their size, excess stress causes our buckets to overflow and is a sign that something needs to change.

In a nutshell
Our physical and mental response to demands or pressure that are greater than our ability to cope.

Why it matters
Too much stress can cause physical and mental health problems. Learning about it and how to cope with it can help us feel less overwhelmed.

Key figures
Thomas Holmes & Richard Rahe
Ian Roberston, b.1951
Hans Selye, 1907–1982

Make the connection
nocebo effect, p.19
flashbacks, p.62
the big five, p.115

burnout

The term 'burnout' was coined in 1974, by German-born American psychologist Herbert Freudenberger, in his book, *Burnout: The High Cost of High Achievement*. It is not a medical diagnosis (although it is probably the cause of other medical and psychological conditions, like depression or anxiety), but is recognized as a specific type of stress linked to the workplace. It is mental and physical exhaustion caused by prolonged strain.

Symptoms of burnout include lack of motivation; feeling cynical, useless and exhausted; and reduced effectiveness at work. Achieving at a high level does not necessarily lead to burnout. If stress and workload are well managed, we probably won't experience burnout. Some workplaces are more prone to it – medicine, nursing and teaching are some of the most notable burnout professions. During the Covid-19 pandemic, reports of burnout and compassion fatigue increased substantially, especially in schools and hospitals.

Research has shown that the main factors working to prevent burnout are people's own levels of personal resilience and social support. Looking at burnout on an individual level ignores the wider context, like poor pay, for example. According to a 2018 Gallup report, five workplace factors contribute to employee burnout: unreasonable time pressures; lack of communication and support from management; lack of role clarity; unmanageable workload; and unfair treatment. Organizational interventions like flexible working, job redesign and wellness programs can help to ease the problem.

In a nutshell
A state of mental and physical exhaustion. It can happen when we experience long-term stress, particularly in demanding workplaces.

Why it matters
Burnout causes physical and mental harm, affecting our lives outside the workplace.

Key figures
Herbert Freudenberger, 1926–1999
Christina Maslach, b.1946
Gordon Parker

Make the connection
moods/emotions, pp.66–7
mirror neurons, p.141
brain scans, p.150

melancholia

From the Greek meaning 'black bile', this term stems from Ancient Greek philosophy and medicine, and Hippocrates' theory of four, separate personality types – the sanguine, choleric, melancholic and phlegmatic, defined by the relative dominance of four 'humours'.

Today, melancholia is described as a persistent and deep state of sadness, despair and emotional numbness. A person might be diagnosed as having depression with a subset of melancholic symptoms. The main features here are pervasive anhedonia, or lack of interest in anything, psychomotor retardation (slow thinking or movement), unreactive mood, early-morning waking and loss of appetite and weight.

Psychoanalytic treatments for melancholia explore the unconscious conflicts, early childhood relationships and experiences that underlie negative symptoms. The idea is that emotional processing can be facilitated through therapeutic empathy, insight and self-compassion. Cognitive behavioural approaches for melancholia focus on challenging negative automatic thought patterns, increasing behavioural activation and teaching coping strategies. Psychiatric treatments are antidepressant medications to alleviate symptoms. More often than not, people with melancholic depression undergo all three treatments at different stages.

In a nutshell
A complex mood disorder consisting of a persistent state of deep despair and sadness.

Why it matters
Melancholic people struggle with the trials of daily life. Understanding melancholia will help us all to develop insight and adaptive coping strategies..

Key figures
Denis Diderot, 1713–1784
Sigmund Freud, 1856–1939
Thomas Holloway, 1800–1883

Make the connection
counsellor/clinical psychologist, pp.8–9
anxiety/depression, pp.88–9

I've given up.

languishing

Sociologist Corey Keyes coined the term 'languishing' in the early twenty-first century to describe a psychological state characterized by a feeling of emptiness, lack of meaning and purpose. He said that symptoms include a lack of motivation to do anything and a general sense of numbness. Languishing seems like depression but is different. It falls on a continuum between depression and what Keyes calls flourishing. People who are languishing are able to function, but feel disconnected from their passions and experience a general sense of apathy or disengagement.

Languishing is not a diagnosable disorder. It may be affected by factors like social isolation, unfulfilling relationships or work, lack of social support and stress. Similarly, life events, financial worries and a general lack of interest in the world may contribute to languishing. People who are languishing sometimes describe not feeling like themselves. they have lost their 'va va voom', their joie de vivre.

Ways to combat languishing, apart from talking therapies, are to have a change of scene or even take a different route to work if that shakes things up a bit. Giving yourself permission to enjoy things and building in a 'playdate' with yourself can help counteract boredom. All the usual self-care techniques like meditation, journaling, exercise, yoga and gratitude can also help.

In a nutshell
Can be thought of as the absence of good mental health, with a lack of engagement and a general sense of dissatisfaction.

Why it matters
Languishing can prevent us from really enjoying our precious time on this earth. Psychology can offer useful tools to help overcome this state of apathy.

Key figures
Adam Grant, b.1981
Corey Keyes

Make the connection
procrastination, p.57
emotions, p.67
anxiety/depression,
pp.88–9

guilt

This emotion is characterized by self-blame, and a feeling of remorse from having done something bad or a perceived sense of having done something wrong.

Guilt plays an important role in how we handle relationships and our own psychological wellbeing. It can influence all aspects of our thoughts, feelings and behaviours.

Psychoanalytic theory delves deeply into the concept of guilt. It is seen as an intrapsychic conflict between the superego – our highly moral voice – and the id – our primitive instinctual drives. Sigmund Freud said that guilt is a useful mechanism whereby we can regulate our behaviours and maintain a healthy society. Guilt helps us stick to societal norms and ethical principles. Psychoanalysts propose, however, that unresolved guilt leads to neuroses and other psychological distress.

Guilt can be learned through role modelling and socialization. It often runs through generations and cultures. Albert Bandura's 1977 social-learning theory emphasizes the importance of imitation and modelling on the feelings of others. Perhaps Grandma feels very guilty for not providing a hot meal for the whole family every night; she feels that she has damaged her family and is inadequate. The attitude is observed and unwittingly learned by daughter and granddaughter and continues through generations, creating a family culture characterized by female guilt.

In a nutshell
A self-conscious feeling of distress about our potential responsibility for doing or saying something with negative outcomes.

Why it matters
By understanding how guilt impacts on our relationships we can restore a sense of self-worth and pride in ourselves.

Key figures
Martin Buber, 1878–1965
Sigmund Freud, 1856–1939
Alice Miller, 1923–2010

Make the connection
id, p.10
Sigmund Freud, p.30
neuroticism, p.71
hedonism, p.73

shame

Whereas guilt is concerned with the feeling we get when we have done something wrong, shame is the feeling we get when we believe that there is something fundamentally wrong with our whole selves. It *can* be related to a particular event or behaviour, but this is not always the case.

Feelings associated with shame are self-disgust, a sense of inadequacy and perceived violations of social norms. Evolutionary psychologists believe that shame plays a role in the survival of our species because it makes us adhere to social and cultural norms, creating better societies.

Psychodynamically speaking, shame is an internal psychic conflict arising from the discrepancy between an individual's ideal self and their actual self-image. Unresolved shame can lead to the creation of defence mechanisms like denial, avoidance and projection. In the workplace, for example, you might feel completely ashamed and embarrassed for entering the wrong data in a spreadsheet and, in a bid to cover up the shame, you try to conceal your error or project it onto someone or something else, blaming your tools for your bad workmanship! This exacerbates inadequate feelings and creates a vicious cycle of disconnection from others, leading to more shame and more disconnection.

There is increasing evidence that serious problems like addictive behaviours and self-harm occur when shame is deeply woven into a person's sense of self.

In a nutshell
The humiliating feeling of distress that we experience when we believe that we are, or that we have done, something inherently wrong.

Why it matters
If we can examine our difficult feelings of shame and share them openly, we can realize we are not alone with them and enhance our own feelings of self-worth.

Key figures
Alain de Botton, b.1969
Brené Brown, b.1965
Carl Jung, 1875–1961

Make the connection
psychotherapy, p.102
anxious attachment, p.125
bystander effect, p.135

envy

Envy is a negative emotion occurring when we long for what someone else has, who they are or what they have achieved. Envious people often feel insecure, inferior and hostile towards those they envy. Sometimes they may not be aware of it, or may be reluctant to admit it, because envy is an ugly emotion and is socially unacceptable.

But envy is a completely natural process, often beginning in childhood with siblings competing for attention and comparing how they are treated by their parents.

'Penis envy' is a concept embedded in Sigmund Freud's psychosexual stages of development. It was heavily criticized by psychoanalytic thinkers like Karen Horney, a neo-Freudian, who proposed the idea of 'womb envy' as an innate male psychological trait.

Where feelings of envy interfere with our lives, therapy can be effective. Exploring the nature of envy, when it appears and why, can shed light on our own genuine goals and desires.

In a nutshell
That uncomfortable feeling we have when we desire the advantages of other people. It can lead to us feeling bad about ourselves.

Why it matters
Talking therapy can help us to address complex emotions like envy, facing them head on and therefore diluting their power, for a less hostile world.

Key figures
Charles Darwin, 1809–1882
Sigmund Freud, 1856–1939
Frans de Waal, 1949–2024

Make the connection
grief, p.74
psychiatric medication, p.103

jealousy

Most of us use the words jealousy and envy interchangeably. Yet psychologists agree that there are distinct differences between the two emotions. Jealousy generally refers to feelings and thoughts of fear, insecurity and worry over the potential *loss* of something.

Unlike envy, jealousy usually involves three parties. We feel threatened that someone else will take away someone or something that we already have – jealousy of your partner's sexy colleague is a straightforward example. So, jealousy, unlike envy, does not always involve a sense of inferiority; it is more concerned with competition and losing out.

If jealousy is so intense as to interfere with daily functioning, therapy can help. Couples therapy, cognitive behavioural therapy, dialectical behaviour therapy and psychotherapy can all help us to understand the process of jealousy, its underlying causes and how to manage the feelings. We can then develop strategies and skills to help us better manage the situations and personalities that trigger our jealousy.

In a nutshell
The fear of losing something valuable to a rival. We want to keep what we have rather than coveting what someone else has.

Why it matters
It is useful to know about the psychology of jealousy, as it is a common emotion that can frighten us. When it is intense and overwhelming, it can lead us to behave rather badly.

Key figures
Luise Eichenbaum, b.1952
Sigmund Freud, 1856–1939
Susie Orbach, b.1946

Make the connection
emotions, p.67
love/attraction, pp.128–9

IT'S MINE!

qualitative research

Qualitative research is used to understand someone's social reality, attitudes, beliefs and experiences. It is widely used in psychology, where much of what is studied is subtle and subjective. Qualitative research looks closely at the interpretation of non-numerical, descriptive data.

In psychology, qualitative research is used to explore insights into our lived experiences and contexts. These methods allow nuance, complexity and diversity to come to the fore. They are, however, criticized for being easily influenced by researcher bias, difficult to fully replicate, and lacking in rigour.

There is a range of research methods under the umbrella term of qualitative research. Phenomenological inquiry is where the unique phenomena of meanings are unpacked and explored; grounded theory allows research psychologists to create new conceptual frameworks though analysis of data; narrative analysis looks at how we tell our stories and how we make sense of our experiences; ethnographic research, usually observational, immerses researchers in naturalistic settings.

In a nutshell
Involves non-numerical and in-depth data analysis, rich in detail and context.

Why it matters
Qualitative research offers valuable methods for data analysis, theory making and in-depth understanding of psychological concepts.

Key figures
Virginia Braun & Victoria Clarke
Paul Felix Lazarsfeld, 1901–1975
Jonathan Smith

Make the connection
moods/emotions, pp.66–7
forensic psychology/criminology, pp.110–11

quantitative research

Qualitative research usually asks 'why' or 'how?', while quantitative research tends to ask 'what?' questions: 'What happens when ... ?' It involves the collecting and analysing of numerical data to test hypotheses.

Quantitative researchers examine relationships and patterns in data to explain human behaviours and emotions. Because the data is numerical, quantitative research methods can be used to test theories, taking a narrow and specific approach. These methods are supposedly less prone to bias than qualitative research. A powerful psychology experiment that used both quantitative and qualitive analysis was the 1961 Stanley Milgram experiment on obedience, in which Milgram, a psychologist at Yale, tested the willingness of participants to administer an electric shock to volunteers. ('What happens when ... they are told to administer shocks?') He used quantitative analysis to show that 65 per cent of participants were willing to deliver the maximum level of electric shock. By noting down comments and behavioural responses, however, he also used qualitative analysis to answer the questions 'why?' and 'how?'

'Quantitative' is an umbrella term. Underneath it sit all approaches to do with measuring, including psychometric surveys and experimental research in which variables are manipulated to assess cause-and-effect relationships. These methods prioritize generalizability, objectivity and statistical inference.

In a nutshell
Quantitative research methods involve analysis of numerical date.

Why it matters
High-quality quantitative research allows hypothesis-testing, establishing patterns and drawing evidence-based conclusions.

Key figures
Ronald Fisher, 1890–1962
Charles Spearman, 1863–1945
Ernst Heinrich Weber, 1795–1878

Make the connection
mental health/mental illness, pp.68–9
mind/brain, pp.154–5

The numbers show ...

habit

Do you bite your nails? Engage in late-night snacking? Or do you regularly go jogging? Whether positive or . . . less positive, these are all habits - repeated behaviours that become automatic over time. The common feature of all habits is that we do them without awareness or conscious intention. Habits are deeply engrained patterns of behaviour, learned through repetition and reinforcement.

Psychologists believe that habits are controlled by a neurological loop with three sub-components: cue, reward and relief. The cue is the trigger that starts off the habit: having a cup of tea might be the cue for eating a sweet biscuit. The reward and relief might be the feeling of comfort, feeling less hungry, or a sugar high from the biscuit. The reward and relief themselves are reinforcing. With repetitions and over time - cup of tea plus the reward and relief of that sweet biscuit - the behaviour becomes automatic. If you have one, two, three biscuits after that cuppa, you enjoy them less - you get used to it - this is called habituation.

Habit formation and behaviour-change work are the nuts and bolts of what many practising psychologists do. Techniques like substituting behaviours (having a carrot instead of a biscuit), creating new rewards (doing something really special instead of having a biscuit or a carrot) and distraction (listening to music) help to break habits.

In a nutshell
Habits are repetitive behaviours that we learn though repetition and reinforcement.

Why it matters
Habits impact on our daily behaviours and long-term achievements.

Key figures
Ivan Pavlov, 1849–1936
B. F. Skinner, 1904–1990
Edward Thorndike, 1874–1949

Make the connection
operant/classical conditioning, pp.22–3
confirmation bias, p.48
nature/nurture, pp.116–17

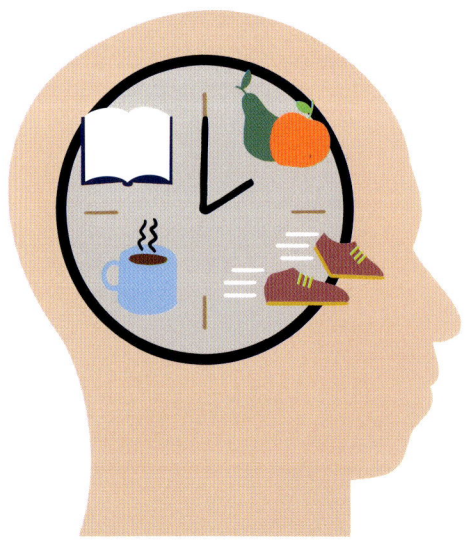

addiction

Both habits and addictions are behaviours that become automatic over time. The difference is that we can, ultimately, take or leave habits, but this is much harder for addictions, to the extent that they interfere with our everyday lives. An addiction is the *compulsive* engagement with a behaviour, even if it has adverse effects on your health or wellbeing.

You can be addicted to pretty much anything. 'Healthy' addictions include running, going to the gym or knitting; addictions to gambling, drugs, sex, doom scrolling or damaging relationships are considered more negative. The main issue is that they disturb us or others around us, and we are unable to stop. In this sense, there are no 'healthy' addictions.

The mechanisms that create addictions are both physiological and psychological. The physiological part happens through the hijacking of the brain's reward system. Dopamine (the 'happy hormone') is released in response to a behaviour. When this happens, we feel good and we will want to repeat that behaviour (run, have sex, sing), to make us feel good again. The psychological component is that we get addicted to things as a result of stress, anxiety or emotional pain. The addiction, whatever its form, helps to distract us from the pain. Addictions usually involve a loss of control, cravings and withdrawal symptoms when the object of addiction is removed.

In a nutshell
Repeated, negative habits that become entrenched and unhelpful.

Why it matters
Addictions can be destructive, leading to distress and unhappiness in ourselves and our loved ones. Understanding the mechanisms of addiction can help us to alleviate the problem.

Key figures
Ivan Pavlov, 1849–1936
B. F. Skinner, 1904–1990
Edward Thorndike, 1874–1949

Make the connection
motivational interviewing, p.108
twins, p.118

anxiety

Anxiety is a complex emotional and physical state consisting of fear, apprehension, sweating, palpitations, worry and generally feeling agitated. It is a normal human response to threat and was actually very useful to us in prehistoric times, alerting us to the presence of predators, for example. Heightened sensitivity to peril meant we were able to protect ourselves in the face of danger.

On the other hand, anxiety that is always there, out of proportion or highly persistent, can significantly impair emotional wellbeing and spoil our quality of life. This happens when people have the physical and emotional symptoms of anxiety even when there is no actual threat present. This kind of anxiety is on the increase in the West and anxiety disorders like panic disorder, phobias and social anxiety disorder are experienced by many, especially since the Covid-19 pandemic and with the increase in social media use.

People who suffer with anxiety disorders have severe physical symptoms like a racing heartrate, sweats and dizziness. These symptoms are due to the activation of the body's stress-response system. Cortisol and adrenaline hormones are released into the body to help us respond to perceived threats. All too often these threats are just that – perceptions – but the process kicks in nonetheless. If anxiety is impacting on your life, CBT or other talking therapies can help you to see things differently, reducing the frequency and intensity of anxiety experiences.

In a nutshell
An emotional and physical response to threats real or perceived.

Why it matters
Anxiety can be debilitating and is on the rise among young people. We need to know more to understand how to combat this epidemic.

Key figures
Aaron Beck, 1921–2021
Albert Ellis, 1913–2007
Russ Harris, b.1962
Hans Selye, 1907–1982

Make the connection
moods/emotions, pp.66–7
psychotherapy, p.102
cognitive behavioural therapy, p.105

depression

'Aaaagh, I feel so depressed!' Statements like this have become part of our everyday talk. But clinical depression is much more than a low mood. It is persistent feelings of sadness and hopelessness, and loss of interest or pleasure in all activities. Not only do depressed people feel flat and low mentally, there are usually also physical ramifications. Depression is often accompanied by changes in appetite and sleep, and reduced energy levels.

There are several different kinds of depressive disorder, including persistent depressive disorder and perinatal depressive disorder. Another kind is seasonal affective disorder, in which people are unable to function in the darker winter months. There is often a link between depression and other psychological issues like self-harm, anxiety and obsessive compulsive disorder (OCD). When depression exists at the same time as another disorder, the causal direction, if one exists, can be unclear. Does the OCD cause the depression or does the depression cause the OCD? In a sense it doesn't matter, as long as the person is helped with all of their problems.

Depression is commonly thought to go hand-in-hand with creativity, though a number of psychological studies investigating the connection have failed to find clear-cut answers.

Paradoxically, clinicians have found that art and creative activities can be valuables outlet for feelings of despair and stress. It is complicated!

In a nutshell
A complex and debilitating condition of mental ill health, characterized by feelings of sadness and hopelessness.

Why it matters
60 per cent of those who take their own lives have had a recent episode of depression; finding effective treatments is critical.

Key figures
Aaron Beck, 1921–2021
Peter Lewinsohn, 1930–2022
Martin Seligman, b.1942

Make the connection
Sigmund Freud/Carl Jung, pp.30–31
melancholia, p.78
obsessive compulsive disorder, p.90

obsessive compulsive disorder

OCD is a mental-health condition. Sufferers are plagued by intrusive thoughts (obsessions) and repetitive acts (compulsions). These can interfere to an extreme extent with daily living.

A person with OCD ruminates about events or people. Usually to alleviate these painful anxieties, they carry out compulsive behaviours. There is a kind of magical and irrational thinking that goes on: 'If I check the front door ten times, then nothing bad will happen to my family.' Common compulsive behaviours are checking, cleaning, counting and arranging objects. While many of us show some of these behaviours, someone with OCD feels the urge to carry out a certain behaviour over and over again, to the extent that the condition interferes with life and can cause other mental-health problems like depression.

Treatment is typically a combination of cognitive behavioural therapy, exposure and response prevention, where a person has to face their fear (of dirty hands, for example) and feel it without carrying out the compulsion (washing). Medication and general talking therapies are also effective treatments.

Often compulsive thoughts and behaviours can be a response to very real traumatic events and are not so irrational when put into context. The condition can emerge at any time in life, including childhood. A combination of genetics, neurological, cognitive, familial and environmental factors are thought to be among the possible causes.

In a nutshell
A mental–health condition in which sufferers repeatedly think about distressing thoughts or events and carry out compulsive and ritualistic behaviours to alleviate the distress of these thoughts.

Why it matters
Some estimates say that about 1 per cent of the population suffers at times from symptoms of OCD.

Key figures
David M. Clarke, b.1954
Stanley Rachman, 1934–2021
Paul Salkovskis

Make the connection
psychotherapy, p.102
cognitive behavioural therapy, p.105
nature/nurture, pp.116–17

perfectionism

Perfectionists have incredibly high standards in every area of life and are overly critical of themselves and how they perform, experiencing great distress when they fail to meet their own standards. There are some similarities with OCD, but arguably more differences. Perfectionism stems from a desire for success and achievement, unlike OCD, which is more about preventing bad things from happening.

As with OCD, many people have perfectionist tendencies to some degree. Such traits include fear of failure ('What will happen if I get this wrong?'), highly critical thinking ('I am useless, why can't I do this properly?') and all-or-nothing thinking, when almost perfect equals total failure! Perfectionist personalities tend to experience more shame and guilt than other people when things don't go right. They find it hard to let go and often procrastinate for fear of not being perfect – they avoid even starting that essay, because what if it turns out to be rubbish?

Therapists and psychologists work with perfectionists when they hit insurmountable obstacles in life. The causes of perfectionism can be multifaceted and tend to centre on low self-esteem, overcritical parenting, a need for control and fear of judgement from others. Of course, in real life there is no such thing as 'perfect'. Being imperfect is part of the human condition, so being a perfectionist is a constant uphill struggle.

In a nutshell
A character trait that leads people to hold unrealistic expectations for themselves and others.

Why it matters
Unhealthy perfectionism can lead to unnecessary worry, anxiety and feelings of depression.

Key figures
Wayne Goodman
Michael Jenike, 1945–2023
Judith Rapoport, b.1933

Make the connection
anxiety, p.88
cognitive behavioural therapy, p.105

autism spectrum disorder

For many neurodivergent people, their autism is their superpower. Actor Anthony Hopkins and activist Greta Thunberg are just two of the high-profile figures to have shared their autism diagnoses. Autism spectrum disorder (ASD) is a neurodevelopmental condition characterized by difficulties with expressing and reading emotions, communication challenges and repetitive behaviours.

It is known as a 'spectrum' disorder because the severity of symptoms can vary greatly. At one end of the spectrum, people with ASD may have no language, exhibit behaviours like hand flapping and rocking, and require supported living. At the other end, they might need to stick to routines and focus on details, dates and numbers. Sensory sensitivity – for example, heightened sensitivity to sound, noise or the feel of clothes on the skin – can also be a part of the condition for some people.

Autism may be diagnosed in childhood or later on in life. It is currently more prevalent in males than females, though the number of females with autism is on the rise, with females presenting symptoms quite differently to males. The exact cause of autism is not known. Help, if needed, can take the form of cognitive behavioural therapy, applied behavioural analysis, speech therapy, occupational therapy and social skills training.

In a nutshell
A diagnosis characterized by differences from the general population in the areas of social skills, communication, rigidity, repetitive behaviours and specific, almost obsessive interests.

Why it matters
While there is no cure for ASD, knowing you are not alone and using appropriate interventions to manage life can help.

Key figures
Leo Kanner, 1894–1981
Lorna Wing, 1928–2014

Make the connection
clinical psychologist, p.9
neurodiversity, p.14
traits, p.112

attention deficit hyperactivity disorder

Like autism, attention deficit hyperactivity disorder (ADHD) is a neurodevelopmental disorder. However, it presents quite differently from autism. It is characterized by persistent patterns of inattention and impulsivity – doing or saying something without thinking about it – and hyperactivity. Most people with ADHD are easily distracted, struggle to stay on task and can show behaviours like excessive talking or fidgeting.

ADHD is thought to be caused by a disruption in the brain's executive function. The executive function, a bit like the conductor in an orchestra, organizes our brain's cognitive processes. In ADHD the executive function does not operate smoothly – the conductor can't keep time – and this can cause emotional dysregulation.

There is a widely held misconception that those with ADHD can never focus. This isn't exactly the case; if someone with ADHD finds an activity intrinsically motivating, they may show hyper-focus, sometimes called 'perseverative responding', where they are totally absorbed and can easily tune out everything else.

It is thought that more than 6 million children in the USA have been diagnosed with ADHD.

Strategies that help people with ADHD include: planning the day ahead, setting boundaries, breathing exercises for stress, medication and talking therapies.

In a nutshell
A neurodevelopmental disorder; it presents as emotional dysregulation, lack of attention and lack of impulse control.

Why it matters
With cases on the rise, and controversy surrounding the causes and treatments of this condition, we need to work hard on understanding more about it.

Key figures
Russell Barkley, b.1949
Joseph Biederman, 1947–2023
Stephen Hinshaw, b.1952

Make the connection
neurodiversity, p.14
traits, p.112
electroencephalo-graphy, p.151

borderline personality disorder

Doctors previously thought that this disorder was on the 'borderline' of two other, different disorders – neurosis and psychosis. Nowadays this term is considered a little outdated and it is usually called EUPD (emotionally unstable personality disorder). It is marked by an instability in mood, a changeable self-image and difficult relationships. People with BPD or EUPD regularly fall out with others; they fear abandonment and often alternate between the idealization and denigration of other people. They can experience severe emotional dysregulation and lose their tempers at the flick of a switch. They struggle with a sense of who they are.

BPD/EUPD has been a controversial diagnosis since it was formalized on the DSM-III (Diagnostic and Statistical Manual of Mental Health Disorders – the authoritative guide to the diagnosis of mental disorders) in 1980. It is criticized for its weighted construction – that it is a label given to 'hysterical women' – its inconsistent meaning and its stigmatizing application.

BPD/EUPD cannot be cured outright and there are no medications that treat it directly, but people can learn to manage the way it manifests. A particular mode of talking therapy called dialectical behavioural therapy (DBT) is highly recommended. It involves teaching mindfulness and bringing awareness to emotional and behavioural patterns. Mentalization based therapy (MBT) and schema focused therapy (SFT) are also used to help with BPD.

In a nutshell
A mental–health condition for life, characterized by unstable moods, emotional dysregulation and difficult interpersonal relationships.

Why it matters
Psychologists and others can help people manage these difficult feelings and associated complicated relationships.

Key figures
Peter Fonagy, b.1952
Otto Kernberg, b.1928
Marsha Linehan, b.1943

Make the connection
mindfulness, p.50
resilience, p.70
traits, p.112

bipolar disorder

It's easy to muddle these conditions because bipolar disorder also involves mood swings, instability and impulsivity. In reality, however, the two are very different.

The main distinction lies in the nature and style of these mood swings. In bipolar disorder, mood shifts between extremes of utterly high and manic feeling (hypomania) and deep lows and depression. Unlike BPD/EUPD sufferers, people with bipolar disorder have a pretty solid sense of self outside of their mood episodes. Their mood episodes last a while and take a while to change (sufferers experience, perhaps, several shifts in a year) unlike those of people with BPD/EUPD, whose moods can switch quickly from day to day.

Bipolar disorder used to be called manic depression. When people are in a manic phase, some report loving it and feeling at their best – alive, creative and productive. As with depression, there are many well-known creatives who suffer with bipolar disorder: Mariah Carey, Selena Gomez and Robert Downey, Junior, to name just a few. At the same time, however, manic episodes can be associated with poor decision-making, like going on shopping sprees or engaging in risky sex.

Episodes of mania or depression can be influenced by external circumstances, like the seasons or even pregnancy. In some people bipolar disorder can tip into psychosis and suicidal ideation.

Psychiatric medication and talking therapy are the main treatments for bipolar disorder, although episodes can recur throughout life.

In a nutshell
A mental-health disorder characterized by mood swings over time: happy and high to very low and depressed.

Why it matters
Extreme episodes of bipolar disorder are disruptive for sufferers and their loved ones and can lead to problems at work and home. It is worth getting to grips with how it works and what can alleviate symptoms.

Key figures
Ellen Frank
David Miklowitz
Kay Redfield
Jamison, b.1946

Make the connection
psychosis, p.101
psychotherapy/
psychiatric
medication, pp.102–3

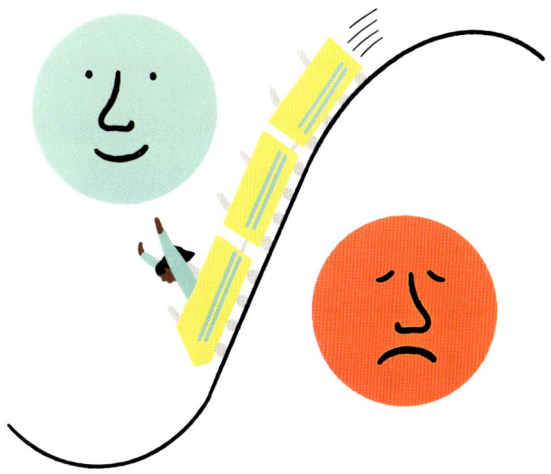

flow states

Imagine you are swimming in a race; attention is focused on the movements of your body, your breath, the power of your muscles and the feel of water on your skin. You are living in the moment, absorbed in the swim. Time seems to fall away. You are tired, but you barely notice. This is an example of a flow state, characterized by complete absorption in, and focus on, a single activity.

Mihaly Csikszentmihalyi was the Hungarian-American psychologist who coined the term 'flow' to describe this focused presence.

Flow states occur when there is balance between a sense of control and mastery. Being 'in flow' can have huge benefits for mental health and wellbeing. When we are in this state we have enhanced creativity, motivation and productivity. Flow is connected to emotional regulation, skills and performance.

It is suggested that in a flow state there is less activity in the prefrontal cortex of the brain. The prefrontal cortex is normally connected to self-consciousness and higher cognitive function, so this could well explain the sense that there is an absence of time and consciousness when we are in flow. Another theory, synchronization theory, suggests that different regions of the brain communicate with each other more freely in a flow state. Other research has found that there is an increase in dopamine (the 'happy hormone') when in flow. All or some parts of these theories may be true.

In a nutshell
Flow is being 'in the zone', immersed in a state of focus, completely absorbed in a task with some level of mastery.

Why it matters
Knowing about this special state can help us identify the activities and environments that are best for our mental health.

Key figures
Mihalyi Csikszentmihalyi, 1934–2021
Katalin Hefferon
Susan A. Jackson

Make the connection
moods, p.66
resilience, p.70
the unconscious, p.147
mind, p.154

psychedelic trips

Like flow, a psychedelic trip is an altered state of consciousness in which we lose track of time. But that is about the only similarity between the two concepts. This altered state of consciousness is induced by substances like LSD, DMT or psilocybin (magic mushrooms).

Psychedelic trips usually involve enormous changes in perception, emotion and cognition; they can be intense hallucinatory experiences involving vivid imagery, sounds or smells and a change in the sense of self or reality. You can experience your own birth or death, or the loss of your ego, while your consciousness embraces the whole of existence. You can feel – maybe for the first time in a long time – a profound and true love towards yourself and to all living creatures.

The exact nature of a psychedelic trip varies between individuals and is influenced by individual difference, setting and dosage. Psychedelics were used in psychotherapy in the 1960s, but changes in social attitudes and politics halted their use until very recently. New research suggests there can be profound healing and therapeutic benefits in using psychedelic trips to treat mental-health conditions like depression or PTSD. In controlled settings, use of psychedelics can lead to deep insights and shifts in perspective, promoting psychological growth and wellbeing. Right now, hallucinogenic drugs are being used therapeutically and the treatment outcomes are being evaluated. This could be the future medicine for mental ill health.

In a nutshell
Psychedelic trips are altered states of consciousness produced in our brains through the ingestion of hallucinogenic drugs.

Why it matters
Medical 'trips' form a new direction for talking therapies and psychiatry, and may have significant impacts for people who suffer from chronic mental ill health.

Key figures
Robin Carhart–Harris, b.1980
Roland Griffiths, 1946–2023
Stanislav Grof, b.1931

Make the connection
flashbacks/hallucinations, pp.62–3
emotions, p.67

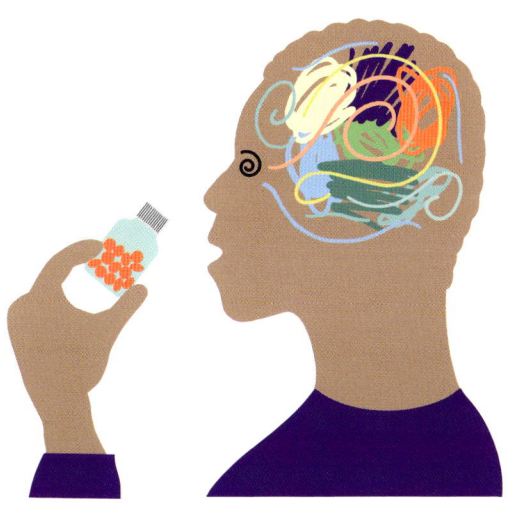

amnesia

Henry Molaison is a well-studied case of amnesia. In around 1953 Molaison underwent experimental neurosurgery to help his epileptic seizures. The operation worked on his seizures, but it also led to his subsequent amnesia – he lost his memory. Interest in him was so intense that following his death in 2008, Molaison's brain was donated to science and the process of brain sectioning was streamed and viewed online.

Amnesia is a word of Greek origin, meaning partial or complete memory loss. It affects short- or long-term memory and can be temporary or permanent. The causes of temporary amnesia include concussion, high fever, emotional stress, drugs or electroconvulsive therapy (ECT). Head injury, trauma, drug use and conditions like Alzheimer's are potential causes of longer-term amnesia.

There are many different types of amnesia. In global amnesia, memory loss is sudden and temporary, lasting from a few hours to a day. You are fine one moment, but the next have no idea who you are, where you are or why. Retrograde amnesia happens when memories of events prior to the amnesia are lost. Anterograde amnesia (the kind Molaison developed) is an impaired ability to form new memories after the onset of amnesia.

Treatment for amnesia depends on its underlying cause. But there will usually be an element of rehabilitation to improve cognitive function: playing memory games, card games, making and memorizing shopping lists.

In a nutshell
A general term used to describe memory loss, both short-term and permanent.

Why it matters
Memory is a crucial part of daily life, affecting speech, learning and all our daily activities.

Key figures
Brenda Milner, b.1918
Daniel L. Schacter, b.1952
Endel Tulving, 1927–2003

Make the connection
memory/forgetting, pp.40–41
Alzheimer's disease, p.152

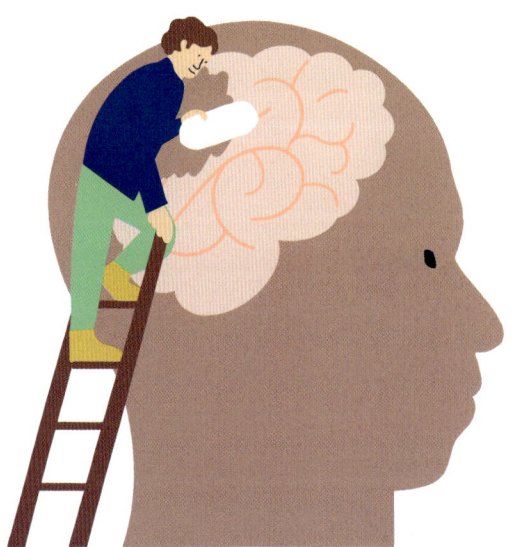

dissociative identity disorder

This is a complex psychological condition; people who have it experience two or more personality traits. If you have DID you may feel as if different aspects or states of your identity are in control of your behaviour and thoughts at different times. Each of your identity states may have different patterns of thinking and relating to the world.

It is safe to say that the majority of people who develop dissociative identity disorders have experienced repetitive trauma in childhood, ranging from persistent bullying to severe abuse. Dissociation is a way of switching off – cutting out all the bad and distressing experiences to which you have been subject.

Unlike amnesia, which is memory loss, DID is memory *disturbance* and is often accompanied by a sense of identity being fragmented. While amnesia usually manifests as an inability to recall past events or experiences, DID is to do with the presence of distinct and separate identities, each with *their own* memories and behaviours.

Treatment for DID is often psychotherapy, which can encourage someone to feel safe, helping them to stabilize in their identity. CBT can help with difficult behaviours and thoughts. Eye movement desensitization and reprocessing (EMDR) can also help with specific traumas and alleviate symptoms.

In a nutshell
A psychological condition that manifests in lost memories and distinct separate expressions of the self that operate within one person.

Why it matters
Dissociation is a way to deal with extreme psychic and emotional pain. Understanding how it works can help people who suffer it with healing.

Key figures
Onno van der Hart, b.1941
Elizabeth Howell
Richard Kluft, b.1943
Colin A. Ross, b.1950

Make the connection

schizophrenia

'Dementia praecox', meaning early dementia, was the term created by Dr Emil Kraepelin in the late 1800s to describe what we now know as 'schizophrenia'. The condition was entangled with ideas of fear and violence and with scary negative stereotypes. Dr Jekyll and Mr Hyde, the Joker, *Psycho* – literary and pop culture has continued to influence how many people think of the condition. But the stereotypes are problematic.

In reality, schizophrenia is a severe and chronic mental disorder, generally characterized by symptoms like hallucinations, delusions (both of these are also symptoms of psychosis), impaired social functioning and disorganized thinking. Many who are not familiar with the condition assume that the voices are nasty and hostile, but sufferers of schizophrenia have reported making friends with their voices and using them as comfort.

Psychiatrists talk about positive and negative symptoms of schizophrenia. Positive symptoms tend to be behaviours that 'add' something, like hallucinations or delusions. Negative symptoms, by contrast, take away – anhedonia is a loss of enjoyment in things, avolition is a lack of desire to do anything. The general public tend to fear those who suffer schizophrenia, and often this is due to some alarmist media coverage. Contemporary research shows that just 5 per cent of people convicted of murder in England and Wales were diagnosed with schizophrenia. For most sufferers, OCD, anxiety, voices and suicide attempts are associated with the condition.

Medical treatment, CBT, support and campaign groups (the Hearing Voices Network in the UK) mean that people can manage their schizophrenic symptoms and be highly useful members of society.

In a nutshell
A mental-health disorder with a range of distressing symptoms, including hallucinations, delusions and disorganized thinking.

Why it matters
People who suffer with schizophrenia can lead meaningful lives when they receive proper support.

Key figures
John G. Csernansky, 1954–2022
Irving Gottesman, 1930–2016
Robin Murray, b.1944

Make the connection
mental illness, p.69
psychiatric medication, p.103
cognitive behavioural therapy, p.105

psychosis

Psychosis is a symptom of schizophrenia, with which it is closely connected, but it is also a symptom of other mental-health conditions. It is not clear cut, but schizophrenia has many phases, which can last from weeks to years. Psychosis is more of a discrete, singular occurrence, rather than an evolving illness

Psychosis happens when you interpret reality in very different ways from those around you. It can be diagnosed if you persistently see or hear things that are not there (hallucinations) or believe things that are not true (delusions). Unlike schizophrenia, which is a condition for life, a psychotic episode can be a one-off event. Or people can have repeated episodes of psychosis throughout their lives. It can occur in conjunction with many kinds of mental disorders, like severe depression, bipolar disorder or paranoid personality disorder. Some women even experience psychotic episodes after childbirth.

First episodes of psychosis tend to occur in young people between the ages of 18 and 24 years and the problem is usually spotted through severe mood and behavioural changes – extreme mania or depression.

A few studies have shown that childhood trauma (particularly childhood sexual abuse) may be more prevalent in those with a diagnosis pf psychosis. So, treatment must involve knowing what *happened* to a person instead of simply diagnosing what is *wrong* with them. This treatment usually involves a combination of medication, talking therapies and social support. Often specialist teams are able to offer early interventions.

In a nutshell
Psychosis happens when people lose touch with reality. It may occur as a one-off episode or sporadically through life. Psychosis can be a symptom of schizophrenia or associated with other mental disorders, or not.

Why it matters
Early intervention in psychosis can prevent recurrence and help those who suffer with it.

Key figures
David H. Barlow, b.1942
Richard Bentall, b.1956
John Read

Make the connection
self–talk, p.34
depression, p.89
mind/brain, pp.154–5

psychotherapy

White man with beard and glasses? Lying on the couch while a money-grabbing therapist analyses your crazy dreams? These are the common stereotypes of psychotherapy. In reality it is about a unique talking and listening relationship between a trained professional and another human who is in psychological distress.

Today 'psychotherapy' is essentially another word for talking therapy. It provides a supportive and non-judgemental environment where people can explore thoughts, feelings and behaviours. Talking in psychotherapy is not like talking with a friend or family member. A therapist has no agenda of their own; they are separate from your world and they are trained to truly listen, to be on your side – even if that means challenging you. They link what they hear about your story to psychological theory and research. Through this unique therapeutic relationship, people gain insight into their circumstances and develop coping strategies to help with difficulties.

There are lots of different types of psychotherapy – cognitive behavioural therapy, psychodynamic therapies – and regular counsellors sometimes describe themselves as therapists. The main difference between counselling and psychotherapy is that counsellors tend to help people with immediate issues in the here and now, whereas psychotherapists look at long-term, historical issues and deeper growth. Whatever the school of talking therapy, research findings show that it is *how you click* with your therapist – the therapeutic alliance – that makes all the difference to outcomes. Different forms of talking therapy have been shown to be highly effective in helping with issues such as anxiety, depression and grief.

In a nutshell
A talking therapy aimed at helping people cope with emotional difficulties and more complex mental–health problems.

Why it matters
With stress and anxiety on the rise, psychotherapy offers a place where people can seek support for mental challenges.

Key figures
Jerome Frank, 1889–1957
Bruce Wampold, b.1948
Irvin Yalom, b.1931

Make the connection
Sigmund Freud/ Carl Jung, p.30–31
motivational interviewing, p.108
the unconscious, p.147

psychiatric medication

Psychiatric medication and psychotherapy are both primary treatments for mental-health difficulties and disorders, and are frequently used together. The difference is that psychiatric medications act directly on neurotransmitter systems in the brain. Neurotransmitters are the body's chemical messengers. They carry information across the space from one nerve cell to the next nerve, muscle or gland cell. These messages help you feel sensations and respond to all the information that you receive from other internal parts of your body and from your environment. Psychiatric medication alters the way information is interpreted and experienced in your brain, mind and body. It eases symptoms of anxiety, depression or mood instability. Selective serotonin reuptake inhibitors (SSRIs) – like fluoxetine, aka Prozac – do this for depression, and antipsychotic medications like risperidone work on psychotic symptoms.

Psychiatric drugs have become part of our daily lives. Prescribing psychiatric medication is a fine art, though – not all medications work in the same way for everyone. Also, psychiatric medication does not cure a condition, though it helps stabilize mood and can help symptoms go away.

There is a body of criticism against psychiatric medication, particularly in relation to the gross profits of the pharmaceutical industry. Some argue that it would be more effective to deal with bigger problems – like fragmented living, abuse and poverty – rather than drugging people for a 'quick fix'.

In a nutshell
Psychiatric medication is prescribed to people who suffer with mental–health disorders to alleviate distressing symptoms.

Why it matters
When a condition is really entrenched, psychiatric medication can lift a person's mood so that they can then access other help or make changes in their lives.

Key figures
Peter Breggin, b.1936
Joseph Glenmullen, b.1950
David Healy, b.1954

Make the connection
mental illness, p.69
schizophrenia, p.100

psychodynamic therapy

This is the original form of psychotherapy, as developed by Sigmund Freud in the early 1900s. Although this type of Freudian therapy is often mocked and (mis)characterized in films and media, it can be a valuable way into our psyches to help psychological healing.

Through weekly (or more frequent) sessions, the therapy explores how unconscious thoughts and past experiences influence recent behaviours, feelings and relationships. The idea, in essence, is that our past informs our present, whether we like it or not and whether we are aware of it or not.

Psychodynamic psychotherapy specifically focuses on the unconscious mind, which, Freud said, contains repressed thoughts, emotions and memories that act on and through our present selves. The psychodynamic therapist will work with a client, using techniques like dream analysis and free association, to explore these unconscious processes.

All of these ideas are based on the work of Sigmund Freud and the very many others who followed him. The idea is that healing, recovery and growth happen when we gain insight into underlying dynamics. By doing this we create healthier coping mechanisms, improve self-awareness and are able to live more meaningful lives. This form of therapy is used to treat a range of conditions, from mild discomfort to depression, anxiety and severe mood disorders. The length of the work can vary from 12 sessions – brief psychodynamic psychotherapy – to longer therapy that may last years.

In a nutshell
The type of talking therapy derived from the theories and psychoanalytic practice of Sigmund Freud – a way into exploring the unconscious.

Why it matters
By being more aware of what drives us to think, feel and behave as we do, we can create happier relationships with ourselves and our loved ones.

Key figures
Sigmund Freud, 1856–1939
Otto Kernberg, b.1928
Melanie Klein, 1882–1960

Make the connection
mood/emotion, pp.66–7
resilience, p.70
anxiety/depression, pp.88–9

Tell me about your childhood.

cognitive behavioural therapy

Like psychodynamic therapy, cognitive behavioural therapy (CBT) looks to improve our wellbeing by exploring thoughts, feelings and behaviours. CBT, however, deals with this in a much more conscious and structured way. It does not go far back into a person's past history, nor into their unconscious.

Aaron Beck, the father of CBT, was originally a psychiatrist and then a psychoanalyst. Growing increasingly frustrated with both psychoanalysis and behavioural theory, he developed the theory and practice of CBT in the 1960s. Clients are often given homework tasks and practical exercises to help them enhance their daily lives: tasks like behavioural activation (clients perform certain activities and then 'monitor' them to assess their impact on moods and thoughts) or cognitive restructuring (in which a person's negative thoughts are restructured).

CBT is a more rigid course of therapy than psychodynamic therapy, lasting for between 6 and 12 and sometimes up to 20 hourly sessions. It is widely used in the USA, UK and Europe, with hundreds of outcome studies showing its effectiveness. Some of these findings should be taken with a pinch of salt, however, as they do not account for revolving-door cases, i.e., clients who come back for help again and again. CBT has also been criticized for its emphasis on technique, rather than on the importance of attentive listening. For many people, however, it is a valuable treatment and an introduction to the world of thoughts, feelings and the use of emotional language.

In a nutshell
A short, limited course of therapy that helps people with problems by changing the way they think and behave.

Why it matters
CBT is a cost-effective way for dealing with specific problems. It has been highly evaluated and consequently is often the initial treatment of choice for many.

Key figures
Aaron Beck, 1921–2021
David M. Clark, b.1954
Albert Ellis, 1913–2007

Make the connection
classical/operant conditioning, pp.22–3
addiction, p.87
family therapy, p.106

Your homework this week is...

family therapy

Imagine being stuck in a room with your whole family, discussing the ins and outs of who's the favourite, who let you down and even wondering, 'How can I possibly be related to these people?' Make your toes curl? Well, this is the essence of most family therapy sessions.

Family therapy – also known as systemic therapy, working with the whole family system – is a form of talking therapy that focuses on improving communication, resolving conflicts and enhancing relationships between family members. Fortnightly or monthly sessions take place with one or two therapists plus the family: children, parents/step-parents, grandparents and sometimes the family in its widest sense, including good friends or aunties. The therapists will intervene to gently challenge entrenched family beliefs and test out hypotheses about what is going on.

The family system is a bit like a snooker table – one ball moves (due to the father's death, for instance) and this affects the relative positions of all the other balls (the sons move in to protect their mother). Make another hit (the mum meets another guy) and everyone moves around again.

When difficult events – divorce, death, addiction – happen in families, the relationships and behaviour patterns shift in all kinds of weird and wonderful ways. Family therapy can help shift unhelpful ways of relating to one another.

In a nutshell
Talking therapy that works with the family as a whole, providing a space for families to address difficulties together.

Why it matters
Although difficult at times, family therapy can help improve relationships and strengthen resilience.

Key figures
Monica McGoldrick, b.1943
Salvador Minuchin, 1921–2017
Virginia Satir, 1916–1988

Make the connection
developmental psychology, p.24
grief, p.74
anxiety/depression, pp.88–9

couples therapy

Ali and Mo came to couples therapy because they were struggling with Mo being absent every night, lost in his work. Ali was on the point of leaving Mo because he was never around for the small things and the good moments with their new baby. Talking it through with the safe guidance of a skilled outsider, they realized that Mo was feeling redundant and useless; he didn't really know how to be a dad, partly because his own dad had left the nest when he was just two years old. Couples therapy helped them work it all out. The clue is in the name!

Like family therapy, couples therapy works with more than one person as the client. A couples therapist is specially trained to look at the dynamics between intimate partners, acting (more than any other kind of therapist) as a mediator between individuals to help with communication and conflicts. Common issues might be infidelities, conflicts over finances, sexual problems and deceptions. As in family therapy, it can be very challenging for a therapist to 'hold the space' and stay neutral when interacting with more than one person.

This form of therapy usually starts with an assessment phase, where information is gathered and the therapist gets a feel for the two people in the room. The therapy then moves into problem-solving and homework tasks – like date night once a week with no phones!

In a nutshell
Talking therapy that provides a structured and supportive environment for couples.

Why it matters
Improving relationships and resolving conflicts can enable couples to lead emotionally healthier lives, usually together but sometimes separately.

Key figures
John Gottman, b.1942
Sue Johnson, 1947–2024
Esther Perel, b.1958

Make the connection
bonding, p.124
love/attraction, pp.128–9

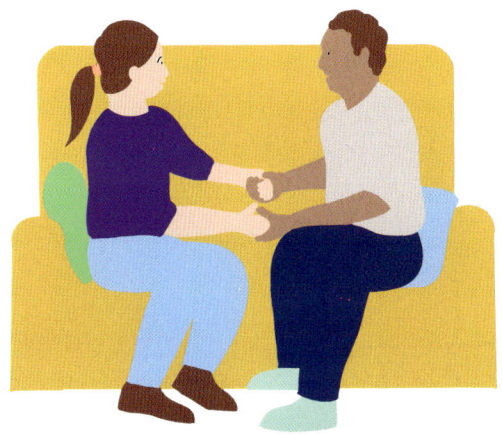

motivational interviewing

Psychologists William Miller and Stephen Rollnick came up with the practice of motivational interviewing (MI) in 1983. It is an approach to counselling and therapy designed to elicit and then strengthen our intrinsic motivation for change. Say, for example, someone with a gambling addiction comes to see their cognitive behavioural therapist. The therapist might initially use motivational interviewing techniques to ascertain exactly how willing they are to change their behaviours.

The therapist will use specific techniques to facilitate change, like open-ended questions ('How does that feel?'), reflective listening ('You are saying that you are frightened'), summarizing ('you are saying that the addiction is getting you really down') and affirmations ('Great work!'). The idea is that the therapist enhances motivation to make positive changes.

MI puts the emphasis on collaboration rather than confrontation or persuasion. No matter how much a therapist wants a client to change their behaviour, it can only, the idea goes, come from the client themselves. The therapist's job is to tease out the motivators for change and build them up so that the recovery process is as easy as it can be for the client.

This is a technique rather than a theory and has been criticized for having no theoretical basis, but, equally, it is helpful because it is pan-theoretical – it can be used by any kind of therapist whatever their school of training.

In a nutshell
A therapeutic interviewing approach that strengthens and empowers a person to change their unwanted behaviour patterns.

Why it matters
MI has been shown to be effective in facilitating behaviour change across substance abuse, weight management and chronic disease management.

Key figures
William Miller, b.1947
Theresa Moyers
Stephen Rollnick, b.1952

Make the connection
counselling, p.8
habit/addiction, pp.88–9

interpersonal therapy

This form of therapy was initially developed in the 1970s by Gerald Klerman and Dr Myrna Weissman as a treatment for severe depression, though it is also now used to treat other mental-health problems. It is based on American psychiatrist Harry Stack Sullivan's interpersonal theory – the idea that interpersonal relationships are the primary driving force in human life.

IPT is a time-limited, attachment-focused and highly structured form of talking therapy. There are usually between 12 and 16 hour-long sessions with a trained therapist. During the first few sessions of IPT, your therapist will learn about your symptoms and goals, clarifying your important interpersonal relationships. Normally the work focuses on role transitions: life changes like getting divorced or becoming a parent. In other instances, the focus is on interpersonal deficits, like problems in the quality of someone's social relationships.

In the next phase, the therapist helps find ways to understand and tackle the identified issues. He or she may use strategies like clarification (identifying patterns), role playing (trying out different styles of communicating) and encouraging affect, which means expressing all emotions – even the ugly, hateful ones that you would rather sweep under the carpet!

MI and IPT are very different types of therapy. MI is all about working out a person's interest in changing and whether they are even ready for it. IPT focuses on the business, the bread and butter of change.

In a nutshell
Focuses on addressing interpersonal challenges and improving social functioning.

Why it matters
A solutions-focused, structured form of therapy, IPT provides effective mechanisms to achieve change.

Key figures
Ellen Frank, b.1944
John Markowitz, b.1954
Myrna Weissman, b.1935

Make the connection
counsellor/clinical psychologist, pp.8–9
psychotherapy, p.102

forensic psychology

By now you will appreciate that psychology has applications in nearly every area of life! Forensic psychology is the study and application of psychology principles in the context of the law, helping us to understand criminal law, the judiciary, criminal behaviours and how people behave on juries and in the dock.

Today, theories in forensic psychology are widely applied in legal contexts. The work of American psychologist Saul Kassin on false confessions, for example, was key to overturning the conviction of the 'Central Park Five', five young men accused of the rape of Trisha Meili in New York in 1989. By using theories relating to the unconscious, bias, group dynamics and eye-witness testimony, forensic psychologists can also use their skills to explain how jurors behave in the trials of convicted criminals.

Perhaps the best known aspect of forensic psychology, however, is psychological profiling – the fascinating process whereby forensic psychologists try and work out the who could be the criminal and why. They do this by looking at the behavioural patterns, motivations and personality traits of a potential suspect. By joining up all this information, forensic psychologists can usefully narrow down the pool of suspects in a criminal investigation, meaning that that the investigating police can focus on the right areas in solving the case.

Nowadays there is no escaping films or TV dramas featuring a clever, witty and often down-trodden forensic psychologist, and these mainstream portrayals may explain the increased popularity of forensic psychology at degree level.

In a nutshell
Applies psychological theories to all areas of the law, the judiciary and to helping understand criminal behaviours

Why it matters
Forensic psychology can help us to understand and predict how people work in crime and punishment settings; this can make for a fairer judicial system.

Key figures
David Victor Canter
Maryanne Garry
Hugo Munsterberg

Make the connection
counsellor/clinical psychologist, pp.8–9

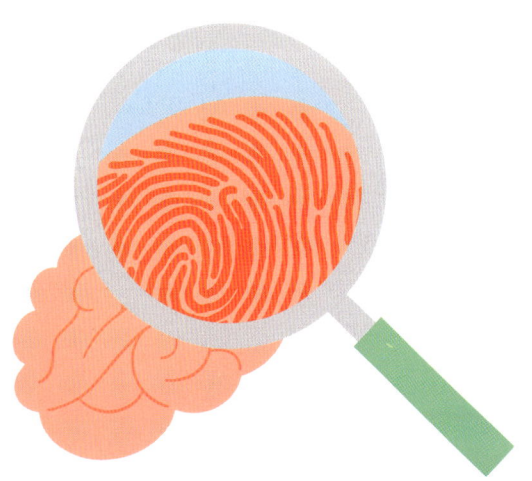

criminology

Both criminology and forensic psychology involve the study of criminal behaviour, but they differ in both focus and approach. Criminology has sociology at its core, and criminologists use sociological theories, rather than psychological principles, as a starting point in understanding the world of crime and punishment.

Criminologists think about how individual behaviour is influenced by social structures, culture and institutional values. Whereas forensic psychologists draw on psychological principles – they deal with the individual mental processes, emotions, relationships and behaviours of criminals – criminologists examine this behaviour in relation to social inequality, power dynamics and social change.

While forensic psychologists work in the police, the NHS, the judicial system or in private practice, criminologists tend to work in academia or research institutions. Criminology encompasses a wide range of topics, like theories of criminal behaviour, crime causation and the effectiveness of punishment and rehabilitation. Criminologists look at trends, big data and societal factors, and can help to shape new policies around crime and punishment.

Both forensic psychology and criminology require a strong understanding of human behaviour. Forensic psychology is more applied and practical in nature, however. Criminology tends to be more theoretical.

In a nutshell
The study of criminal behaviours and our reactions to them on individual or societal levels.

Why it matters
By understanding what leads to criminality, we can start to relate to criminal behaviours so as to reduce them and minimize harm.

Key figures
Mary Gibson
Cesare Lombroso,
1835–1909
Paul Topinard,
1830–1911

Make the connection
mental illness, p.69

crime prevention

causes

rehabilitation

criminality

traits

Traits can be either endearing or infuriating! What are your key personality traits? Do you avoid conflict? Prefer to stay in and be quiet or are you the life and soul of the party? Is your glass half full?

Traits are the characteristics of a person – what makes them who they are across different settings, times and situations. Traits are not entities in the brain, but they represent underlying parts of our personality, influencing how we perceive ourselves and how we interact with others.

Traits are thought to be within us from early on (that is, if you believe that nature rules over nurture). In 1977, Alexander Thomas and Stella Chess suggested, based on their observational research, that babies show temperament styles or traits from birth. They categorized the children, as follows:

- **Easy** These children generally have a positive attitude, are quick to adapt to new situations.

- **Difficult** These children cry more often, have a harder time adapting to new situations, and don't regularly follow routines.

- **Slow to warm up** These children adapt slowly and can react negatively, but show low intensity in their emotional reactions.

Traits can impact on a person's functioning for life. Agreeableness and extroversion are associated with better interpersonal relationships, for example, and may help you at work and in family life. On the other hand, a high level of the neuroticism trait can lead to increased stress and susceptibility to psychological distress.

In a nutshell
A person's general psychological characteristics.

Why it matters
Understanding traits and how they develop and shift can have fundamental effects on how we see ourselves and how others see us.

Key figures
Gordon Allport, 1897–1967
Raymond Cattell, 1905–1998
Robert McCrae, b.1949

Make the connection
neurodiversity, p.14
cross-cultural psychology, p.26
intelligence, p.44
introversion/ extraversion, pp.120–21

social roles

Think of all the roles you play – mother, teacher, husband, friend, daughter. Like traits, social roles define who we are, but, unlike traits, they refer to the set of expectations that society throws at us. Social role theory proposes that everyday activity is a lot to do with the acting-out of socially defined categories. Each role is a set of duties, expectations, rights, norms and behaviours that a person has to face and/or fulfil.

The social role model observes that people behave in predictable ways, and that our behaviours are context-specific, based on factors including social position. Gender roles offer a prime example of this. In days gone by, most women largely stayed in the domestic realm and their social roles were pretty clear – cook, cleaner, mother, carer, no work, no income, no power. Role expectations can be unhelpful and perpetuate societal inequalities. Yet, at the same time, some societal expectations can be helpful, like a binding glue; everybody knows where they are and how to behave. If you start a new job, you will quickly learn about the role you play in that organization and whether it fits with your own personality and expectations.

Stress and tension develop in us when there is conflict in our social roles. Take the simple example of a contemporary working mother in the West. She may have power, independence and autonomy, but the conflicting demands on her time and resources can lead to overwhelming stress and anxiety.

In a nutshell
Social roles interact with traits to shape a person's behaviour and experiences.

Why it matters
People may internalize societal expectations. Understanding the interplay between traits and social roles can offer insights into how we navigate social and work environments.

Key figures
Judith Butler, b.1956
Ralph Linton, 1893–1953
Talcott Parsons, 1902–1979

Make the connection
LGBTQ+ psychology, p.15
cross–cultural psychology, p.26
confirmation bias, p.48
bilingualism, p.58

personality types

'It's just who he is, it's his personality!' Is your personality a fixed entity, rooted in your very being, or can we shift, change and grow? Psychology has been asking this question for centuries.

It all started in ancient Greece with type theory. Hippocrates, and later Galen, broke down personalities into types called 'the four humours'. Each category or humour was also associated with a bodily fluid: yellow bile (ambitious, aggressive, short-tempered), black bile (melancholic), phlegm (cool, calm or unemotional) and blood (sanguine, cheerful, confident). Further down the line, in the twentieth century, this theory was developed by Carl Jung.

At its core, type theory suggests that there are a limited number of personality types. One of the most influential manifestations of this kind of thinking today is the Myers-Briggs Type Indicator (MBTI). This is a test that assigns a binary value within each of four categories: introversion–extroversion, sensing–intuition, thinking–feeling and judging–perceiving. After completing the test, people are given a type like INTJ (introverted, intuitive, thinking, judging) or ESTP (extroverted, sensing, thinking, perceiving). Other tests and descriptions of personality types exist, like the Rorschach inkblot test, in which a person projects his or her own interpretations onto what they see in various inkblot shapes. These tests all offer useful guidelines about what characterizes us, but we should be careful not to believe all they say: personality types are not written in stone ...

In a nutshell
Psychologists have developed many kinds of assessment measures to try and work out which different personality types exist.

Why it matters
With an understanding of personality types, the best combinations of people can work together for the greatest outcomes.

Key figures
Isabel Briggs Myers, 1897–1980
Katherine Cook Briggs, 1875–1968
David Keirsey, 1921–2013

Make the connection
nature/nurture, pp.116–17
Introversion/ extroversion, pp.120–21

What do you see?

the big five

This personality traits model, properly known as the five factor model (FFM), is a widely used framework for understanding personality. It is part of personality theory, categorizing people into realms of personality, but is quite distinct from previous notions of personality types. Developed in the 1980s, it encompasses five broad dimensions that capture different aspects of individual personalities:

- **Openness to experience** Are you curious, imaginative and open-minded? You would score highly on this scale.

- **Conscientiousness** You will score highly on this scale if you are dependable and self-disciplined and if you set high standards and strive for success.

- **Extroversion** You are outgoing, energetic, assertive and talkative; you enjoy excitement and socializing.

- **Agreeableness** You are empathetic, cooperative and value harmonious relationships. If you pride yourself on looking after others, then you will score highly on the agreeableness scale.

- **Neuroticism** You might reflect a tendency to experience negative emotions such as anxiety, depression, stress and worry.

There are other models for understanding personality, but all models are limited in that they do not take account of the widest context and oversimplify the nature of personality.

In a nutshell
A way of measuring and assessing our personalities, emphasizing subtle dimensions of personality rather than discrete categories.

Why it matters
The big five model accounts for context and complexity in helping us understand who we are.

Key figures
Paul Costa, b.1942
Lewis Goldberg, b.1932
Walter Mischel, 1930–2018

Make the connection
Carl Jung, p.31
neuroticism, p.71
birth order, p.119

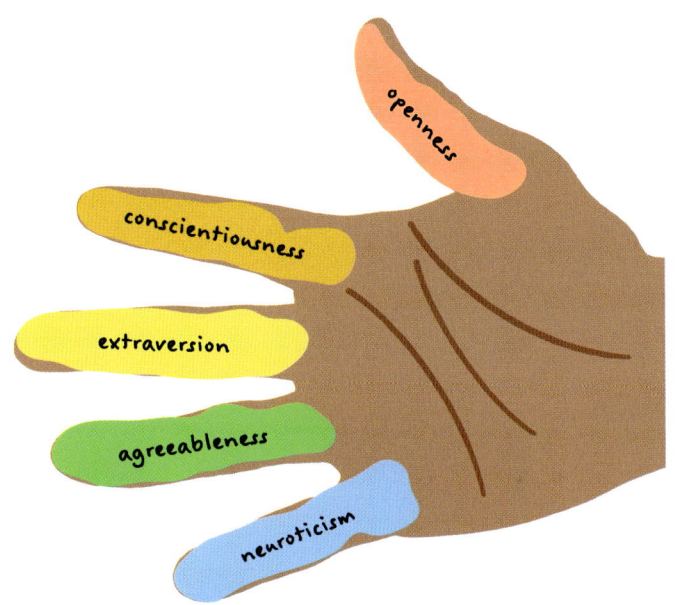

nature

The nature vs nurture question comes to most of us pretty early on in adolescence. How did I turn out like this?! Is it nature or nurture?

In psychology the concept of 'nature' refers to genetics, biology and innate factors that lead us to behave as we do. Drawing on behavioural genetics and evolutionary psychology, nature psychologists study the biological underpinnings that make us who we are.

Evolutionary psychology proposes that many aspects of our behaviour have evolved in response to problems faced by our ancestors. It might be in human nature to fear snakes, for example, even if you have never witnessed a snake or other snake-scared people. Nature psychology would say that this fear has been passed down through generations – that our brains have adapted to include instinctual fear and caution around snakes.

Biological processes involving neurotransmitters, hormones, brain structure and genetics all shape behaviours and cognitions. For example, menopause hormones can affect women's psychology and their behaviours. Research from the UK's Fawcett Society found that one in ten women quit their jobs due to the impact of menopause. Others reported going part-time as a consequence of menopause. These changes were attributed to physical symptoms, as well as to changes in life perspectives. The biological and behavioural are interacting through the psychological to shape behaviours of this specific group. So, nature is important in determining human behaviours and feelings, but it does not exist in isolation.

In a nutshell
The biological influences – genetics, hormones and brain functioning – on behaviours.

Why it matters
It is important to acknowledge the natural underpinnings of our behaviours to avoid overcritical selfanalysis.

Key figures
Francis Galton, 1822–1911
Steven Pinker, b.1954
Edward O. Wilson, 1929–2021

Make the connection
traits/social roles, pp.112–13
personality types, p.114
twins, p.118

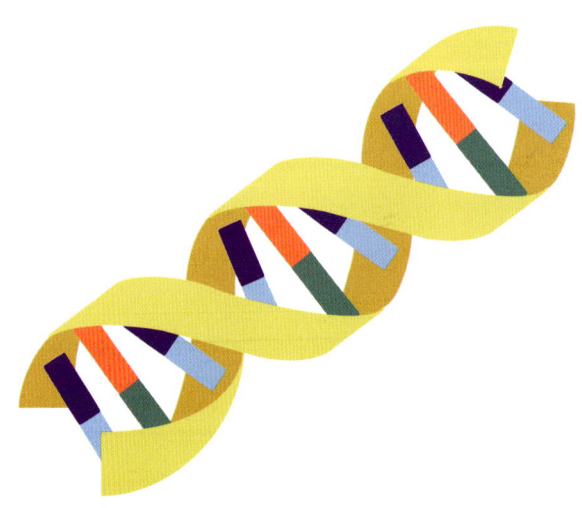

nurture

It can't all be about biology, now can it? After all, we are complex human animals with thoughts, language, feelings and consciousness. 'Nurture' in psychology refers to environmental factors, experiences and social interactions that impact on our development, thoughts and behaviours. Just think about how you were raised. Family culture, ethnicity, religion, education, siblings and friendships will have had a vast influence on making you who you are.

Psychologists spend lifetimes studying the impact of parenting styles, sibling and peer relationships, socioeconomic status, cultural norms and life events on people. Two children, maybe even twins, brought up in the same home environment may have very different lives as adults – why? Due to relationships with their parents, perhaps, or schooling, or culture.

Nowadays psychologists talk about epigenetics – the study of how behaviours and environments can actually alter gene formation – and the biopsychosocial model to conceptualize how nature and nurture interact with each other to shape our personalities and behaviours.

The fascinating and popular UK TV series *Up* is the layperson's peep into the nature-nurture debate. These documentary films – made and broadcast every seven years since 1964, when the participants were seven years old – have followed the lives of ten males and four females from varying backgrounds. Although criticized for its (often dated) assumptions about class and intelligence, there is much food for thought about the interplay between nature and nurture.

In a nutshell
Understanding nurture is the preoccupation of much of psychology.

Why it matters
Understanding nurture – and its best friend, nature – provides valuable insights into the environmental factors that make us who we are.

Key figures
B. F. Skinner, 1904–1990
Lev Vygotsky, 1896–1934
John Watson, 1878–1958

Make the connection
cross-cultural psychology, p.26
personality types, p.114
twins, p.118

twins

With identical twins, scientists know that they are dealing with two individuals with the same genetic make-up, and can investigate environmental influences alone. By comparing identical twins with fraternal (non-identical) twins, psychology researchers examine the relative contribution that genetics and biology and environmental factors can have on personality and behaviour. Twin studies, therefore, seem to offer us a way of finally resolving that nature–nurture debate.

Studies of identical twins have shown remarkable similarities between the two individuals, even when they have been separated from a young age. They show similarities in personality traits, intelligence and temperament. In 1979, Thomas Bouchard, in his 'Minnesota Study' of twins reared apart, found that an identical twin reared away from his or her co-twin seems to have about an equal chance of being similar to the co-twin in terms of personality, interests and attitudes as one who has been reared with them, suggesting genetic factors are crucial.

Another great long-term study called TEDS (the Twins Early Development Study) is being conducted at King's College in London. So far data indicates that, perhaps not surprisingly, genetic *and* environmental influences are important in nearly all aspects of behavioural development.

In a nutshell
Twin studies are an efficient and reliable way for psychologists to investigate the role of nature and nurture in development.

Why it matters
Twin studies provide valuable insights into the development of psychological traits and behaviours.

Key figures
Thomas Bouchard, b.1937
Francis Galton, 1822–1911
Nancy Segal, b.1951

Make the connection
intelligence/ wisdom, pp.44–5
nature/nurture, pp.116–17

birth order

Are you a youngest child, or an eldest? An only child? Think about how it might have affected you. Psychological investigations into birth order offer very different insights from twin studies. Birth order studies suggest that the position of a child in a family can shape their personality, behaviour and even intelligence.

For example, in 2015, a study found that firstborn children had higher levels of intelligence than their younger siblings – perhaps because they receive more individual attention in the early years. But the researchers found no differences between firstborn children and others in terms of broader personality traits like extroversion, emotional stability or imagination. We all know those youngest children who are creative, rebellious and outgoing and who seem to have benefited from flying under the radar of their parents. In order to compete with older siblings, they adapt, using humour to get noticed, or charm, defiance or maybe even resilience.

Middle children are considered by psychologists to be adaptable and diplomatic. They can navigate the dynamic of having both older and younger siblings; they may develop a knack for nurturing relationships. Firstborns can often be responsible and achievement-orientated (Hillary Clinton is an eldest child), showing leadership qualities and a desire for approval.

These are generalizations, of course (oversimplifications, some would say). Genetic differences, life events and unique family dynamics can equally play a crucial role in defining our psychology.

In a nutshell
Psychologists explore and explain the impact that family positioning has on personal psychology.

Why it matters
Our position within our families can greatly affect how our parents treat us and how we develop emotionally and psychologically.

Key figures
Alfred Adler, 1870–1937
Judith Rich Harris, 1938–2018
Kevin Leman, b.1943

Make the connection
moods/emotions, pp.66–7
nature/nurture, pp.116–17
brain scans/electro-encephalography, pp.150–51

introversion

People who are introverted want to be alone; they prefer solitude and quiet environments. Given the choice, they would opt for internal reflection over social interaction. Introverts tend to be more thoughtful, reserved and reflective than extroverts. In a way, introverted people prefer depth of connection over quantity of (perhaps superficial) connections. One way to know if you are an introvert is to take a personality test like the Myers-Briggs Type Indicator (see p.114).

Psychologists and scientists are not sure if there is a specific cause for introversion. Some brain studies have shown a greater flow of blood to the frontal lobe in introverts, which might explain their strengths in problem-solving and planning ahead, though it is not clear whether this feature is a cause or a consequence of the underlying trait of introversion.

You might wonder if your introverted best friend could be socially phobic, but this is rarely the case. Introverts just prefer their own company. In fact, many introverted people have rich inner worlds. They like to explore their own thoughts, create ideas or experiment with hobbies. Interestingly, because they are more reflective, introverted people have been found to have a greater capacity for understanding others. They get it! So if you are feeling a bit emotionally fragile, seek out an introvert to share your problems. They will probably be able to see exactly where you're coming from.

In a nutshell
A personality trait characterized by a preference for alone time, quiet, minimal stimulation and space for self-reflection.

Why it matters
Introversion is a natural aspect of personality with its own strengths and challenges; increasingly we are recognizing what introversion has to offer us as a society.

Key figures
Elaine Aron, b.1944
Jonathan Cheek

Make the connection
the big five, p.115
nature/nurture, pp.116–17
brain scans, p.150

extroversion

This term originates with a spelling mistake! It was originally spelled 'extraversion' (by no less that psychologist Carl Jung, who introduced the concept), from the Latin *extra*, meaning 'outside', and *version*, meaning 'turning'. 'Extrovert' was introduced by mistake in a 1918 paper, but the 'o' version has become a common and popular way to spell it.

The opposite to introversion, extroversion is characterized by sociability, enthusiasm, assertiveness, enjoyment of social interaction – general 'out there'-ness! The extrovert is the one who likes to talk and seek out opportunities for social engagement, is energetic and thrives in social settings.

Extroverted people sometimes get called out for being attention-seeking and egotistical, but it is important to realize that they draw energy from discussing ideas with other people, so they naturally seek out chances to do so. In addition to being outgoing, extroverts tend to be warm and show empathy and a loving attitude towards others. For this reason, they often work in jobs, like public relations, in which communication skills are essential.

As with all personality traits, the nature–nurture question hangs in the air. There are certainly ways you can become more extroverted if that is what you want: visualize social situations, be more intentional in your interactions, push your limits more while also scheduling downtime for yourself.

In a nutshell
A personality trait that characterizes those people who prefer stimulating social environments.

Why it matters
Extroverts are generally thought to have a societal advantage over their introverted counterparts. Nowadays, though, with growing knowledge about the unique attributes of introverts, the division is not so clear.

Key figures
Hans Eysenck, 1916–1997
Jeffrey Alan Gray, 1934–2004
Carl Jung, 1875–1961

Make the connection
traits, p.112
twins, p.118
narcissism/ psychopathy, pp.122–3

narcissism

This term is widely used, but, perhaps, little understood. It originates with the Greek myth of the hunter Narcissus, who saw his reflection in a pool of water and fell in love with it. Longing for this beauty (himself), but never able to have it, he died by the pool's side. People who are narcissists kind of fall in love with themselves, which is as dangerous as the myth makes it sound!

Narcissistic personality disorder, or NPD, is a psychological condition characterized by pervasive patterns of grandiosity, a constant need for admiration and an inflated sense of self. It is important to realize that not everyone who shows signs of narcissism has an NPD. People with NPD exaggerate their abilities, and seek constant admiration and validation from others; they believe that they are special and often show a lack of empathy. They can even go as far as to exploit others to achieve their own goals and maintain their sense of superiority. For example, at work, someone with NPD might engineer a situation so that they take all the credit for the work that someone else has done.

People with narcissistic *tendencies* can show love and develop bonds, but occasionally exhibit selfishness or self-aggrandizing behaviours. Those with an actual *diagnosis* of narcissistic personality disorder show persistent selfishness and can never show empathy. They are unlikely to form deep bonds.

In a nutshell
Behaviour characterized by self-promotion, manipulation and emotional abuse.

Why it matters
Knowing about narcissism can help us to understand what we are dealing with when we see these characteristics in ourselves or another.

Key figures
Sigmund Freud, 1856–1939
Otto Kernberg, b.1928
Heinz Kohut, 1913–1981

Make the connection
anxiety, p.88
psychodynamic therapy, p.104
traits, p.112

psychopathy

The film *American Psycho* (2000) – about a wealthy investment banker who leads a double life as a sadistic serial killer – is a well-known depiction of a psychopath. And movie portrayals, for better or worse, do shape public perceptions of mental illness. In reality, however, psychopathy is a psychological condition characterized by a range of interpersonal affective (i.e. emotional) and behavioural traits including superficial charm, manipulativeness, impulsivity and a disregard for social norms and moral values.

A psychopathic person can often display traits that are narcissistic, but the condition is not the same as narcissism. Psychopathic people can appear completely normal, often charming, but underneath, there is a total absence of conscience and feeling for others. Consequently, psychopaths often engage in criminal behaviour.

Why does someone become this way? Psychological research puts it down to early problems with parent-child attachment. But not everyone who has been abused or suffered from poor attachments turns into a psychopath. So other experts say a person is born that way – the old nature–nurture debate rears its head again. In reality, it's likely that psychopathy is down to a combination of genetics, neurological conditions, adverse parenting and maternal pre-natal risks, like toxicity in the womb.

It is estimated that only 0.6 per cent of the population have psychopathy. Treatment for the condition varies. Some say there is nothing that can be done, but other studies report that CBT is useful for some psychopathic behaviours, like sex offending.

In a nutshell
A severe and chronic personality disorder with significant implications for the sufferer and for society.

Why it matters
In the most serious cases, psychopathy can lead people to commit violent crimes with no remorse. With early treatment, however, psychopaths can get on track and lead functional lives.

Key figures
Hervey Cleckley, 1903–1984
Robert Hare, b.1934
David Lykken, 1928–2006

Make the connection
neuroplasticity, p.27
nature/nurture, pp.116–17
consciousness/the unconscious, pp.146–7

bonding

Sports people do it, choristers do it, lovers do it ... and, of course, babies and their carers do it. Bonding: that unique emotional attachment that forms between two people. Typically, the term is used to refer to babies and carers, but bonding also occurs between children, young people and full-grown adults. Bonding is a fundamental aspect of human development and crucial for emotional wellbeing, social functioning and healthy relationships throughout one's life.

Over the years, many psychologists, doctors and ethnologists have developed theories of bonding and attachment. In 1958, John Bowlby, a British psychiatrist, developed the notion of the affectional bond – the universal human need to seek closeness to another person and feel secure when that person is present. He also developed theories of secure and insecure attachment that are widely used today. American psychologist Harry Harlow's monkey experiments of the early 1960s showed that, given the choice, monkeys bonded with cloth 'mothers' with no milk, preferring them to cold, wire 'mothers' that were holding bottles of milk. The baby monkeys were looking for warmth, softness and contact. Then, in the 1970s, Marshall Klaus and John Kennell, both paediatric doctors, suggested that after a human baby is born there is a sensitivity period for optimal development and bonding; mother and baby should have skin-to-skin contact immediately after birth. This finding is very much used today in hospital maternity units.

In a nutshell
A concept referring to the importance of emotional connection and trust in infancy.

Why it matters
By understanding the process and dynamics of bonding, people can cultivate deeper, more meaningful connections with others.

Key figures
Mary Ainsworth, 1913–1999
John Bowlby, 1907–1990
Mary Main, 1943–2023

Make the connection
grief/separation, pp.74–5
couples therapy, p.107
love, p.128

anxious attachment

Anxious attachment is a form of bonding – but not a particularly healthy one. Have you ever seen clingy children, tied to their parent's 'apron strings', or perhaps to a screen? These children have an anxious attachment style. Adults with anxious attachment styles put great effort into relationships, to the extent of self-sacrifice, and have immense difficulty receiving criticism or rejection.

Anxious attachment is one of four key attachment 'styles' coined by the psychiatrist and psychoanalyst John Bowlby and the psychologist Mary Ainsworth, which are referenced in education and social care, as well as in therapeutic settings. They are:

- **avoidant**, marked by problems of intimacy;

- **anxious**, as described here;

- **secure**, characterized by feelings of safety and trust, and;

- **disorganized**, marked by mixed behaviours of clinginess and avoidance.

Anxious attachments usually develop early. The infant, and later the adult, develops a hyper-awareness of threats to their relationships. But how does it happen? Of course, it might be genetic: babies at four months can show signs of behavioural disinhibition, such as a fast-beating heart and a fear of strangers, which is linked to later separation anxiety. Equally, attachment anxiety can stem from erratic parenting or abuse.

As is often the way in psychology, the idea that these categories are fixed entities, free of cultural and social context, is controversial.

In a nutshell
A form of clinginess that develops in childhood due to erratic and inconsistent parenting (and possibly genetics).

Why it matters
Healthy relationships are based on trust and emotional intimacy. Understanding attachment can help us avoid unhelpful cycles of attachment style.

Key figures
John Bowlby, 1907–1990
Cindy Hazan
Phillip Shaver, b.1944

Make the connection
emotions, p.67
separation, p.75
envy/jealousy, pp.82–3

self-esteem

Feeling you have little control in your life, constantly putting yourself down, finding it hard to reinforce boundaries, engaging in people-pleasing behaviours, comparing yourself unfavourably to others: these are all examples of low self-esteem. Self-esteem refers to our own evaluation of ourselves – our estimations of our self-worth or our capabilities. Self-esteem reflects how confident, competent and worthy of respect we feel.

Lack of self-esteem can lead to all kinds of setbacks – not going for a promotion or entering a competition in a sport you love, for example – but it can also lead to more serious issues like anxiety or feelings of depression. In such instances a vicious cycle can be created, where feelings of depression lead to low self-esteem and low self-esteem creates further feelings of depression, in a spiral of negativity.

Low self-esteem can be put down to many, varying influences – personal relationships, parenting, schooling, sibling relationships, cultural expectations and internal perceptions. Positive experiences like praise and recognition can bolster self-esteem, but this is usually temporary. To build longstanding, healthy self-esteem takes work, like challenging negative beliefs, cultivating self-awareness, setting realistic goals and practising self-compassion. Individual therapy and social support can often help bolster low self-esteem and grow confidence, as can acts of kindness and gratitude.

In a nutshell
A person's own evaluation of their self-worth.

Why it matters
A positive sense of self-esteem is essential to building relationships, achieving goals and, ultimately, to happiness and fulfilment.

Key figures
Nathaniel Branden, 1930–2014
Ralph Waldo Emerson, 1803–1882
Morris Rosenberg, 1922–1992

Make the connection
mental health, p.68
resilience, p.70
happiness, p.72

I am
worth it!

self-efficacy

If your self-esteem is high, then your self-efficacy will be pretty high, too. The two concepts are connected but distinct. Self-efficacy – named by the psychologist Albert Bandura in the mid-1970s – refers to your beliefs regarding your own ability to successfully perform a task, achieve goals or cope with challenges.

Perhaps you just finished a job interview. You really believe you did well because you knew you had prepared thoroughly, you answered the questions well, you learned from feedback given in past interviews, and you know you have the skills to do the job. It just felt good. You have a strong sense of *self-efficacy*.

Our self-efficacy is influenced by a sense of mastery (past successes and failures), vicarious experiences (observing the successes and failures of others), social persuasion (feedback and engagement from others) and, in the immediate term, physiological and emotional states (physical sensations and emotional arousal).

Most people who achieve their desires, who have good psychological wellbeing and function with ease, will have a high sense of self-efficacy. They will be optimistic and believe that they are masters of their own success and satisfaction. Low self-efficacy is associated with experiences of learned helplessness, where you face challenge after challenge, believing that you cannot achieve a successful outcome. Which came first, failure or the belief you will fail? Low self-efficacy can develop as a result of repeated failures or it might be that we get ourselves into situations where we are likely to fail and this then leads to low self-efficacy.

In a nutshell
To do with the beliefs that someone has regarding their own ability to do something well.

Why it matters
Self–efficacy is a useful concept to help us take risks, learn new skills and tackle new challenges in work, play and our relationships.

Key figures
Albert Bandura, 1925–2021
Julian Rotter, 1916–2014
Martin Seligman, b.1942

Make the connection
classical conditioning, p.22
mindfulness, p.50
cognitive behavioural therapy, p.106

I can do it!

love

'My bounty is as boundless as the sea,/My love as deep. The more I give to thee,/The more I have, for both are infinite.' So says Juliet to Romeo in the famous 'balcony scene' of Shakespeare's play. In psychology the definition of love is significantly less poetic. It is defined as a set of emotions and behaviours characterized by intimacy, passion and commitment. It involves care, closeness, protectiveness, attraction, affection and trust. Many say it's not an emotion, but an essential physiological drive.

There are several different theories of love in psychology. The key one – from Zick Rubin, in 1970 – concerns liking versus loving, the distinguishing feature of the latter being that when we *love* someone we care as much about that person's needs as they do their own. So next time you find yourself caring for a sick relative, partner or child, remember this definition. You are living the love!

In 1988, psychologist Elaine Hatfield added to theories of love by proposing that there are two basic types of love: compassionate and passionate. Passionate love happens when we experience heightened physiological arousal in the presence of another person. This love is transitory, according to Hatfield, usually lasting between 6 and 30 months. Ideally, passionate love leads to compassionate love, which is deeper love and care for another person and is far more enduring.

In a nutshell
The key components of love are intimacy, commitment, compassion and physiological responses, which are linked to childhood attachments.

Why it matters
Your feelings about family and friends, as well as even your choice of life partner, may be affected by your experience of love.

Key figures
Mary Ainsworth, 1913–1999
Helen Fisher, b.1945
Robert Sternberg, b.1949

Make the connection
grief, p.74
couples therapy, p.107
bonding, p.124

attraction

Attraction might spark romantic love, but it is very different. Physical attraction is characterized by physiological changes in the body and a release of the chemicals in the brain. Attraction activates the orbitofrontal cortex of the brain, which is the part of your brain that processes sensory rewards. These physiological reactions can manifest in feeling nervous and smiling or unconsciously mirroring body movements.

We assume that attraction starts with looks, but that is not always the case. It can be triggered by intellect, humour, power or anything else. In these instances, physical attraction is secondary.

Psychological experiments have tried to measure attractiveness and its influencing factors. For example, Donald Dutton and Arthur Aron, in their 1974 'bridge' study, found that men who crossed a higher bridge felt more attracted to a female researcher than those who had crossed a lower bridge to greet her. The greater levels of attraction were put down to the participants misattributing feelings of sensory stimulation from the high bridge walking to the female researcher. In another experiment, psychologists asked participants to rate both attractiveness and perceived achievements when looking at a range of different portrait photos. Those faces rated as more attractive were also judged as having lots of other positive attributes – better jobs, relationships and lives. It pays to be attractive, it seems – people will think more highly of you, at first glance at least!

In a nutshell
The physical response to the appeal of another, triggered by the release of brain chemicals and manifesting in changes of behaviours, thoughts and feelings.

Why it matters
It is important to be aware of the physiological and psychological processes involved in attraction, as it impacts on how we treat and are treated by others around us.

Key figures
Arthur Aron, b.1945
Leon Festinger, 1919–1989
Robert Zajonc, 1923–2008

Make the connection
mental health, p.68
flow states, p.96
brain scans, p.150

obedience

'Clean your room now!'
'Why?'
'Because I say so!'

At its core, obedience stems from socialization in childhood: parents, teachers, religious leaders all tell us what to do and how to behave. To some extent, society needs a level of compliance from its members in order to function smoothly. But too much deferral to authority can lead to too much social acceptance of destructive behaviours ('I was just following orders!').

Psychologists have found that people comply with authority to avoid rejection, punishment or disapproval from seniors. Stanley Milgram's famous experiment at Yale University is the perfect illustration of this. Participants in the experiment just obeyed orders from 'the man in the white coat', administering fake 'painful' electric shocks to their subjects, despite their screams of pain. The participants were obedient even when it caused harm!

Social psychologists have tried to explain this by saying that we like to defer responsibility to the expert. If the guy in the coat tells us it is OK, it is OK. We see ourselves as mere agents, performing a task. The Milgram experiment was carried out in 1961. It would be nice to think that society is less deferential nowadays. Sadly, though, a more recent replication of the experiment, undertaken in 2009, found that compliance rates were only slightly lower than those found by Milgram and that there was no difference between men and women.

In a nutshell
The psychological mechanism that makes us comply with authority figures.

Why it matters
Blind obedience is dangerous. Understanding obedience is crucial to helping us challenge authority when required, so that we don't act in unethical ways.

Key figures
Solomon Asch, 1907–1996
Stanley Milgram, 1933–1984
Philip Zimbardo, b.1933

Make the connection
developmental psychology, p.24
stress, p.76
self-esteem, p.126

Do as I say!

conformity

Teenagers – usually understood to be the most rebellious, even disobedient age group – can also be the most conformist. They wear the same clothes, speak the same slang, don't want to be different. It's a beautiful paradox, which neatly illustrates the differences between conformity and obedience!

Conformity has no element of power hierarchy, operates on no orders from above. Instead it works through subtle cues and implicit expectations within groups. It is the desire to fit in and gain social approval or avoid rejection. It begins with comparing ourselves to others and then adjusting our thoughts and behaviours to accord with those perceived group norms. Conformity is usually driven by the need for validation – to belong and to be socially accepted. Group size, demographic and bonding impact on conformity behaviours.

The most famous study on conformity was created by pioneering social psychologist Solomon Asch. Groups of participants were given a visual test. They were shown a series of lines and asked to say which one was the longest or shortest. Asch planted stooges in the group to give fake answers. He found that 75 per cent of people conformed and went along with the stooges' answers, even when they knew that they were wrong! Asch found that when participants gave their answers privately there was less conformity. He came to the conclusion that, in group settings, most people conform. Such findings have dramatic implications for all kinds of environments, particularly juries, governments, wars, terrorism and, on a different level, reality TV programmes.

In a nutshell
The process whereby we adjust our ideas and attitudes to align with group norms or social expectations.

Why it matters
We spend most of our time in groups – we need to know how they work, who is boss, and our role in colluding or standing up for what is not popular.

Key figures
Solomon Asch, 1907–1996
Irving Janis, 1918–1990
Muzafer Sherif, 1906–1988

Make the connection
confirmation bias, p.48
traits/social roles, pp.112–13

Are we conforming?

loneliness

It wasn't so long ago that millions of people across the world were 'locked down' in their homes, many with no companionship, no physical affection and no human interaction. Even without the shock and trauma of illness or death, the Covid-19 global pandemic made many people feel lonelier than ever before.

Loneliness is more than mere absence of social interaction, though. You can feel lonely in a couple, in families or in large groups. Loneliness is a complex and deeply felt emotional state characterized by a profound disconnectedness. It usually brings personal feelings of emptiness, sadness and a lack of belonging, even when other people are around. These feelings can then cause people to withdraw from social life even more. Loneliness is also associated with higher levels of stress and physical ill-health.

In 2018 (pre-pandemic), a large study in the USA found that half of people surveyed reported feeling lonely every single day. The report, by General Vivek Murthy, also found that the risk of premature death due to loneliness increased by 29 per cent when coupled with social isolation.

In short, loneliness is not good for us. The modern shift to online working, virtual shopping and living alone does not always help with combatting the condition. Where possible, we need to get out and get real-life connected. It's not all bad though; online life is a wonderful way to ease loneliness for those who, for whatever reason, struggle to find in-person connections.

In a nutshell
A complicated psychological state of isolation and disconnectedness. It can make us feel sad and lacking in self-belief.

Why it matters
Recent reports suggest that 33 per cent of the world's population is lonely. An astonishing 50 per cent of Brazil's population described themselves as lonely.

Key figures
John Cacioppo, 1951–2018
Louise Hawkley

Make the connection
emotions, p.67
couples therapy, p.107
interpersonal therapy, p.109

solitude

When was the last time you had a moment of peace and quiet? What did you do in your solitude? Did you fret and worry? Did you switch on the TV or scroll on your phone? Or did you embrace the solitude and listen to music, read a book, meditate, walk alone? Solitude is similar to loneliness in that it is a state of being alone. The difference is that solitude is a deliberate choice.

When we seek solitude, we are looking for space away from the busy world outside. We are looking for personal reflection, relaxation or the opportunity to exercise creativity. In contrast to loneliness, solitude can be an enriching, connecting experience.

Some people avoid solitude, keeping themselves busy for every minute of the day. For them, solitude can mean boredom or facing 'demons' – painful feelings of anger or sadness. For others, the conscious decision to rejuvenate, away from the demands of social interactions, means solitude feels like a gift. How we experience solitude is therefore rather subjective.

So the main difference between solitude and loneliness is to do with your perceptions of it and societal expectations. One day you can be solitary and feel great about it; on other days, less so. Psychologists suggest that by developing a balance between solitude – intentional time alone – and social activities, we can cultivate resilience, self-reliance and a deeper sense of joy and fulfilment.

In a nutshell
The intentional choice to be alone with your own thoughts and feelings.

Why it matters
It is important to have time alone to experience our own ideas and enjoy self-reliance.

Key figures
Sara Maitland, b.1950
Anthony Storr, 1920–2001
Robert Yin

Make the connection
procrastination, p.57
anxiety, p.88
self-efficacy, p.127

altruism

Did you help someone out today? Put money in a charity tin? Share your lunch with a colleague? These are acts of altruism. Altruism is that selfless concern, kindness or act of caring that you offer towards other people. It comes under the category of what psychologists call 'prosocial' behaviour, i.e., actions that benefit other people, no matter what the motive. In some cases, acts of altruism lead people to sacrifice themselves just so that they can help others. Why?

Evolutionary psychologists are convinced that altruistic behaviours are undertaken, not out of the goodness of one's heart, but for the collective survival of the species and reproductive success. Altruism happens, according to this theory, because of natural selection – 'survival of the fittest'. If we want to survive as a species we have to work together, and being altruistic facilitates this process. This links to genetic relatedness theory, which states that if you are genetically connected to another, you are more likely to help them. Maybe this is an inherent reason for nepotism. Another reason for altruism is the reciprocal effect ('I'll scratch your back and you scratch mine!'). When we are altruistic, according to neuropsychologists, particular brain reward centres are stimulated. These brain reward systems make us feel good. This leads us to repeat those altruistic behaviours, because it makes us feel good. Not so selfless after all!

In a nutshell
Prosocial, kind and compassionate behaviour, whereby we put other people's needs before our own.

Why it matters
Altruism is arguably one way to measure individual and social health and wellbeing. We consider it a sign of a healthy, well-functioning community.

Key figures
Daniel Batson, b.1943
Martin Nowak, b.1965
E. O. Wilson, 1929–2021

Make the connection
positive psychology, p.29
wisdom, p.45
social roles, p.113

bystander effect

Almost the opposite to altruism, the bystander effect happens when we, knowingly or unknowingly, ignore the needs of others. It is a psychological phenomenon that occurs when, in a critical situation, we don't intervene – we just sit, or rather *stand*, by. We have all seen it: someone is being harassed on public transport and no one says anything, not even you! Why would that be the case?

Social psychologists put it down to several mechanisms. Firstly, the diffusion of responsibility: on a train, for example, where there are other people, we feel less personally responsible for what is going on. We kind of assume someone else will get stuck in.

Secondly, social influence: while a situation unfolds, we look to what other people are doing (see 'Conformity', p.131, and the Solomon Asch experiment). If others are not taking any action, then we think that we don't have to either.

Thirdly, there is what is termed 'pluralistic ignorance': 'I didn't know, I didn't realize they were upset.' Some people occasionally genuinely don't realize how the bullying is impacting on the victim and so they do nothing.

The bystander effect means any of us can collude with cruel behaviours, from watching someone kill a fly, to abuse on a grand scale or even murder.

In a nutshell
A psychological phenomenon: we are less likely to intervene in a situation when there are other people about.

Why it matters
Through awareness of the bystander phenomenon, we can increase the chances of helping others in critical situations.

Key figures
John Darley, 1938–2018
Harold B. Gerard, 1923–2003
Bibb Latané, b.1937

Make the connection
family therapy, p.106
traits, p.112
prejudice, p.138

emotional intelligence

First there was IQ, the intelligence quotient for smart people, then there was EQ or EI, the emotional intelligence quotient, for feeling people. Some experts believe that, for true success in life, the need for high EQ far outstrips the need for high IQ. Emotional intelligence is our ability to interpret, perceive, control, evaluate and use emotions in a constructive and effective way.

Dan Goleman, American psychologist and researcher, is the father of emotional intelligence, but the concept, termed 'emotional strength' by Abraham Maslow, first emerged in the 1960s. EI means: recognizing and interpreting body language, facial cues, tone of voice and language, and understanding the complex interplay of a multitude of feelings, motivations and behaviours.

EI also means coping with our own emotions in adaptive ways, so that we can manage stress, control impulses and maintain resilience in the face of challenges. Effective emotion management allows us to navigate difficult situations in a balanced way. People who have high emotional intelligence can discern the reasons behind emotions and also empathize with the perspectives of others.

The internet abounds with informal questionnaires that promise to assess your emotional intelligence, but two well-known and validated tests are the Mayer-Salovey-Caruso Emotional Intelligence Test and the Emotional and Social Competence Inventory (ESCI). Scores on these tests are useful because they predict success in various domains like leadership, teamwork and mental health.

In a nutshell
The ability to tune in to the emotions of others and ourselves and then react appropriately and sensitively.

Why it matters
Being able to deal with the complex web of emotions in ourselves and our close ones is helpful for functioning in the world of relationships.

Key figures
Reuven Bar-on, b.1944
Daniel Goleman, b.1946
Peter Salovey, b.1958

Make the connection
intelligence, p.44
cognitive reappraisal, p.65
emotions, p.67

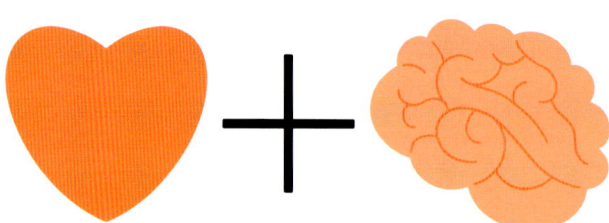

theory of mind

Four-year-old Jimmy is devastated because the wheel fell off his toy truck. He looks sad. His nursery friend Luke offers comfort with his teddy bear. Luke has theory of mind, the capacity to think about the mental state of others and to recognize that other people's perspectives may differ from your own. Theory of mind is just one aspect of emotional intelligence.

Theory of mind starts to develop between the ages of three and five and grows as children become more familiar with the world; through stories, role play and social interactions they learn about how thinking and feeling influence social interactions. Even between the ages of six and eight theory of mind is not fully formed. Most people get there by adulthood.

Some do not. Researcher Simon Baron-Cohen and his colleagues have connected theory of mind to autism, suggesting that, generally, people who have autism spectrum disorders do not have theory of mind. In his study comparing people with autism against others in a theory of mind task, only 20 per cent of autistic people showed they were able to see things from another person's perspective.

There are several false-belief tests to assess theory of mind. The Sally-Anne test is a well-known children's test using dolls. Children with theory of mind are able to understand that, when a marble is hidden while Sally-Anne is out of the room, she will not look for it in the correct place when she returns.

In a nutshell
Not everyone has a theory of mind. Those who do are able to see things clearly from another point of view.

Why it matters
Having theory of mind has practical implications for education, social competence and interpersonal relationships across one's lifespan.

Key figures
Simon Baron–Cohen, b.1958
Joseph Call
Uta Frith, b.1941

Make the connection
neurodiversity, p.14
autism spectrum disorder, p.92
altruism, p.134

prejudice

Sexism, classism, homophobia, ageism – the list of ways in which humans discriminate and are discriminated against is, sadly, endless. Discrimination is perpetuated by prejudice, a social phenomenon involving negative attitudes and stereotypes held regarding other people, based on their membership of a particular group.

Social psychologists try to work out what makes people invest in these stereotypes. For instance, cognitive theories of prejudice talk about cognitive bias and schemas as a foundation of prejudice. Cognitive schemas are mental shortcuts that organize information from our social worlds in our brains. We categorize groups in certain ways, influenced by the media, people around us and an in-group/out-group mentality.

In the 1970s psychologists Henri Tajfel and John Turner came up with social-identity theory, according to which being part of a social group can give you a sense of belonging, self-worth, purpose and identity. Belonging to a social group leads to in-group self-categorization. Self-categorization leads to favouritism regarding one's in-group and hostility towards the out-group.

Affective theories of prejudice highlight the roles of fear, anxiety or resentment in shaping attitudes towards out-groups. In addition, societal factors like historical patterns and injustices lead to disparities in opportunity between groups of people. In order to overcome prejudice, we can benefit from education and contact with those who are different from us on individual and societal levels.

In a nutshell
A set of attitudes that support, cause or justify discrimination. Prejudice is a tendency to overcategorize.

Why it matters
In order to counter prejudice and promote equality, we need to understand the conditions that give rise to prejudice and the psychology behind it.

Key figures
Gordon Allport, 1897–1967
Jane Elliott, b.1933
Henri Tajfel, 1919–1982

Make the connection
confirmation bias, p.48
shame, p.81
bystander effect, p.135

contact theory

The other side of the prejudice coin in psychology is contact theory. Like prejudice, it is a prominent concept within social psychology. It sounds simple: interpersonal contact between different social groups can cut down prejudice and improve inter-group relations under certain conditions. The theory was developed by American psychologist Gordon Allport in the 1950s, but still applies today.

Positive interactions between different groups of people can foster empathy, dispel stereotypes and promote a better mutual understanding. If we work with different people from 'other' groups, we get to know them and reduce our ignorance around them, building bridges.

However, there must be key conditions for effective contact to work – equal status, support from institutions and chances for meaningful interactions. If not, then the prejudices will rise up again. But where contact is 'safe' it can lead to reduced anxiety, increased empathy and more positive attitudes to 'out-group' members.

The theory and practice of contact has been used effectively in all kinds of race relations or inter-ethnic conflict programs in schools and colleges. It could maybe even work with footballing rivals – or maybe not!

In a nutshell

The contact hypothesis suggests that inter-group contact under appropriate conditions can effectively reduce prejudice between majority and minority group members.

Why it matters

If we have contact with and learn about different 'categories' of people, we will modify our beliefs and exhibit less prejudice.

Key figures

Gordon Allport, 1897–1967
Elliot Aronson, b.1932
John Dovidio

Make the connection

social roles, p.113
conformity, p.131
social identity, p.142

empathy

'I understand your frustration', 'I get it, I'm here for you', 'You must feel so conflicted' – all statements that make another person feel understood. Empathy is the ability to understand and share in the feelings and experiences of others. It involves not only recognizing and acknowledging someone else's emotions, but also experiencing a sense of connection and concern for their wellbeing.

Empathy is a fundamental part of human interaction and helps us to bond, cooperate with each other, build friendships and work together to create a functioning and compassionate society. Without it we wouldn't be human!

There are two main elements of empathy. Cognitive empathy is when we logically know how another person feels or thinks. We know, in a practical and factual sense, that other people have thoughts, feelings and perceptions different to our own. Affective empathy is slightly deeper and happens when we feel another person's joy or sadness (or any other emotion) as our own. If someone tells you about the death of their sibling, for example, and you feel tearful, you are really sharing their emotions – 'feeling it' for them.

Empathy is an essential ingredient in good therapy and counselling. Carl Rogers, the father of humanistic counselling, named it as one of the core conditions of any counselling relationship. But empathy is also a key part of all prosocial behaviours (behaviours that benefit other people).

In a nutshell
Our capacity to understand and *feel* another person's perspective. It can move us to act in altruistic ways.

Why it matters
By growing empathy in ourselves and our children, we can reduce intolerance and strengthen the world through kindness and compassion, because we get it!

Key figures
Daniel Batson, b.1943
Martin Hoffman, 1924–2022
Carl Rogers, 1902–1987

Make the connection
counsellor, p.8
positive psychology, p.29
psychotherapy, p.102

mirror neurons

Mirror neurons are brain cells that fire both when we perform a specific action and, incredibly, when we see someone else performing that action. They were discovered in the early 1990s by Italian neuroscientist Giacomo Rizzolatti and his colleagues, whose work lead to mirror neurons being dubbed 'the most hyped concept in neuroscience'!

Brain-imaging experiments (fMRI) show that the inferior frontal cortex (front-bottom-ish part of the brain) and superior parietal lobe (top-back-ish) activate when a person performs an action and sees someone else doing it. These brain regions contain what has been defined as the 'human mirror neuron system' or the 'monkey see, monkey do' neurons. The system develops in humans before twelve months. Smile at a newborn baby and they will smile back at you; stick your tongue out and they will too; blow a raspberry and voila! All are examples of activated mirror neurons.

Mirror neurons are connected to empathy, because in order for us to feel what another person is going through, or to understand it in a cognitive way, our mirror neurons need to be firing. If your mirror neuron system isn't working well, you might struggle with empathy (which may fit with an autism spectrum disorder diagnosis). Conversely, enhancing the firing of mirror neurons through action observation therapy (a fancy way to say copying) may enable you to improve social skills and emotional understanding.

In a nutshell
Brain cells that activate when we are performing an action but, equally, when we watch someone else perform that action.

Why it matters
Mirror neurons are neurologically fascinating but their action also has implications in our everyday lives, in terms of our capacity for empathy and learning.

Key figures
Marco Iacobini, b.1960
Christian Keysers, b.1973
Giacomo Rizzolatti, b.1937

Make the connection
neuroplasticity, p.27
left brain, right brain, p.148
brain scans, p.150

social identity

How do you define yourself? Builder, father, English, upper class? Social identity is about the groups or communities in which we feel we belong. Take Ruth, an eighty-year-old grandmother. As an older woman in society she will often be patronized and ignored, and assumptions, based on prejudice or unconscious bias, will be made about her physical abilities and opinions. She can feel diminished and excluded. However, when she meets up with her tribe – her walking group or other grandmothers – she is empowered and is part of a team! This is social-identity theory in action.

This theory, developed by Henri Tajfel and colleagues in 1979, describes the circumstances under which social identity is more important than personal identity and outlines the ways in which social identity can influence behaviour. Whereas self-identity is about what makes Ruth different in terms of personality or interests, social identity centres on what makes her similar to others – being an older adult, being a grandmother, being near the end of her life.

Being part of a social group brings security and belonging, as well as a reduction in uncertainty, especially in challenging times. When Ruth's husband died, she got support from other older people in the same position – her tribe had been there, too. When people identify with a group, they gain self-esteem from its success, even if they have had nothing directly to do with its achievements. If you support Arsenal football team, your self-esteem rises when your team wins, even though that win is absolutely nothing to do with you!

In a nutshell

How we categorize ourselves in relation to memberships of different social groupings.

Why it matters

Our social identities influence our prosocial behaviours and can provide us with a sense of belonging and increase in self-esteem.

Key figures

Dominic Abrams, b.1958
Henri Tajfel, 1919–1982
John Turner, 1947–2011

Make the connection

cognitive reappraisal, p.65
traits, p.112
personality types, p.114

birds of a feather

'Birds of a feather flock together' goes the saying. The concept, in psychology, refers to the phenomenon whereby people are most likely to form friendships or alliances with others who share similar characteristics, beliefs, values and interests. People are naturally drawn to those who are like them in some way. This is closely connected to social-identity theory and homophily – the preference for similarity in social relationships.

Michal Kosinki and colleagues, in 2017, had concrete evidence to prove that birds of a feather do indeed flock together. In his research with over a hundred universities, he analysed the digital footprint left on Facebook by participant students and concluded that most people interact with others who are similar to them online.

Essentially, we all develop a sense of belonging through membership of certain groups. Flocking together can have several consequences. It leads to the formation of cliques, echo chambers and in-group biases, all of which can reinforce existing attitudes and beliefs that are already exclusive or marginalizing. Polarization online and in real life around gender-identity politics, governmental politics or even beliefs around terrorism versus freedom fighting is, in part, a symptom of the 'birds flocking together' phenomenon - not helpful. At the same time, however, sticking together with your tribe can foster a sense of support and belonging.

In a nutshell
We tend to gravitate to people who are like us. Sticking together can provide comfort and security, but it can also lead to exclusivity.

Why it matters
This concept provides insights into the dynamics of social networks, group formation and inter-group relations.

Key figures
Mark Granovetter, b.1943
Robert Kahn, 1918–2019
Robert Putnam, b.1941

Make the connection
nature, p.116
extroversion, p.121
loneliness/solitude, pp.132–3

cortex

The cerebral cortex is the CEO of the brain. It is thought to oversee operations and decision-making in the company. The outer layer of the brain's surface, it is in charge of coordinating functions like sensory perception, motor control and emotional regulation. Because of this, it is a focal point for neuropsychology and neuroscience.

Brain research is dependent on new technologies and is developing all the time. At the moment, neuropsychologists are trying to work out if, or how, the cortex manages to manage all of the brain departments and sub-departments. They know that different areas of the brain are responsible for processing specific types of information and that the cortex is coordinating it all: sensory input, language, spatial awareness. There is also some evidence that the cortex is linked to executive function, i.e., planning ahead and meeting goals. But the jury is out about how strong this connection is and which part of the brain, if any, is ultimately in charge. Cortical plasticity, or neuroplasticity – the brain's ability to reorganize and re-fire in response to experience – is another key aspect of brain functioning that neuroscientists are working on right now.

Dysfunctions in cortical regions have been associated with schizophrenia, Alzheimer's disease, depression and autistic spectrum disorders. But there is a lot more to discover about how exactly this works. Hopefully, in the longer term, understanding the neural aspects of these disorders can help with treatment and targeted interventions to improve functioning.

In a nutshell
The outer layer of the brain that controls higher-level cognitive functioning.

Why it matters
Knowing how to intervene when brain deficits occur can save and improve lives.

Key figures
Korbinian Brodman, 1868–1918
Paul Flechsig, 1847–1929
Wilder Penfield, 1891–1976

Make the connection
neuroplasticity, p.27
Alzheimer's/ Parkinson's disease, pp.152–3
brain, p.155

We make the decisions round here!

Executive functioning

limbic system

Whereas the cortex consists of structures on the outer surface of the brain, the limbic system is that complex network of structures that are located deep within the brain. The limbic system plays a critical role in regulating emotions, memory, motivation and social behaviours.

The first evidence for there being a system responsible for emotions was discovered in around 1939, by Heinrich Klüver and Paul Bucy. These two scientists discovered that when monkeys had their temporal lobes (brain areas just behind the ears) removed, they showed extreme and strange behaviours.

Within the limbic system are other sub-departments with different functions: the amygdala, hippocampus, thalamus, and so on. The amygdala is the heart of the brain's emotional system, a key player in the formation of emotional memories and regulation of emotional responses. Next to it is the hippocampus, crucial for memory formation and spatial navigation. If you are hungry, the hypothalamus will be doing its work; if you are aroused, the thalamus is on duty.

Scientists still have very little idea about how the brain actually works. After all, the number of synapses (connections) in one human brain is equal to the number of stars in 5,000 Milky Ways, with every synapse consisting of around 100,000 molecular 'switches'. There is a long way to go.

In a nutshell
The central nexus, deep in the brain. Its job is to integrate emotional, cognitive and physiological processes.

Why it matters
Dysfunction within the limbic system can lead to neurological and psychological disorders, so understanding its purpose and function is helpful for mental and physical health.

Key figures
Heinrich Klüver, 1897–1979
Paul MacLean, 1913–2007
James Papez, 1883–1958

Make the connection
moods/emotions, pp.66–7
nature/nurture, pp.116–17

Primitive urges

consciousness

You are aware of reading this sentence, but perhaps at some point you notice an itch on your foot, a moment of wondering what to eat for dinner, a flash of a fragment of a conversation with a friend? This is consciousness – always shifting and changing. Consciousness is our awareness of our own unique thoughts, memories, feelings, sensations and environments. Essentially, it describes our entire awareness of ourselves and the world around us; if you can describe it in words it is part of your consciousness. It is, by definition, also, wholly subjective.

Consciousness has several biological and social purposes. It allows living beings to choose actions, adapt to new information and make decisions. 'Higher' states of consciousness are often associated with meditation, mindfulness or spiritual experiences, and involve an elevated state of awareness, in which we are able to gain a greater sense of ourselves and our roles in the world. Altered states of consciousness happen when we dream, hallucinate, take psychoactive drugs or are subject to hypnosis. Neuroscientists try and map areas of the brain onto different conscious experiences.

In a nutshell
The subjective awareness of thoughts, sensations, emotions and perceptions in ourselves.

Why it matters
It's everything you can think of! Almost our entire experience of life is shaped by consciousness.

Key figures
Sigmund Freud, 1856–1939
William James, 1842–1910
Julian Jaynes, 1920–1997

Make the connection
dreaming, p.12
hallucinations, p.63
psychedelic trips, p.97

CONSCIOUS

the unconscious

Like consciousness, the unconscious is a stream of mental activity, but, in this case, it runs beneath the surface of conscious thought, shaping attitudes and decisions without our being aware of them. Sigmund Freud, founder of psychoanalysis, suggested a model of mind (colloquially called the 'iceberg model') that consisted of three levels: the conscious, the preconscious and the unconscious (in the iceberg analogy, the vast realm deep beneath the ocean surface).

The unconscious, according to Freud, contains repressed or forgotten memories, primitive instincts and unresolved conflict. In Freud's thinking these unconscious processes influence perceptions, decision-making and all kinds of reactions of which we are seemingly unaware. Have you ever had a slip of the tongue? Called your teacher 'mum'? Or maybe blushed in reaction to something, completely out of the blue? These are all examples, so the argument goes, of the unconscious mind popping up in consciousness. Some psychologists argue that is only through these conscious manifestations, like slips of the tongue or dreams, that the repressed unconscious comes into our awareness.

Although not the same as the theoretical Freudian idea of 'the unconscious', it is worth noting that there are other aspects of human functioning that are completely unconscious too – meaning that they happen automatically. The whole operating system of our body – breathing, going to the loo, the beating of our heart – goes on without our active participation! These are functions of the autonomic or automatic nervous system.

In a nutshell
All those activities that are going on in our minds, brains and bodies without our being aware of them.

Why it matters
Learning about the unconscious shines a light on why we behave, think and feel as we do. Understanding it allows us to unlock new relationships, connections and ideas.

Key figures
Sigmund Freud, 1856–1939
Carl Jung, 1875–1961
Jacques Lacan, 1901–1981

Make the connection
id, p.10
slow/fast thinking, pp.38–9
mind wandering, p.51
psychotherapy, p.102

UNCONSCIOUS!

left brain/right brain

Numbers or art? Intuition or logic? Are you 'left brain'? Or 'right'? According to left-brain, right-brain dominance theory, the two sides of our brain have different functions, the right side controlling expressive and creative tasks, the left side better at numbers, reading and language. It is an outdated theory, however, and many haven't caught on to the fact that it is all a bit of a myth!

Today, students might learn about the theory as a point of historical interest. It first came about through the work of American neuropsychologist Roger Sperry in 1981. He studied brain functioning in people who had their corpus callosum – the bit that joins the two hemispheres of the brain – surgically cut to treat a type of epilepsy. Out of this research came all kinds of claims about left- or right-hemisphere dominance.

Despite its oversimplification, it is important to think about our own brain strengths and weaknesses and what areas we might want to improve. For example, if we have difficulty following verbal instructions (often cited as a right-brain characteristic) we might benefit from writing down instructions and developing better organizational skills.

'We can all benefit from improving our brain health, but first we have to identify what may be working for us, or not, and what areas we may want to exercise in order to make them stronger,' says Rachel Goldman, clinical psychologist.

In a nutshell
Left–brain, right–brain dominance theory, which suggests one side of the brain dominates in some individuals, has permeated popular culture.

Why it matters
The brain's organization is more nuanced than this 'theory' suggests, but it does prompt us to investigate the different functionalities of the brain.

Key figures
Joseph Bogen, 1926–2005
Michael Gazzaniga, b.1939
Roger Wolcott Sperry, 1913–1994

Make the connection

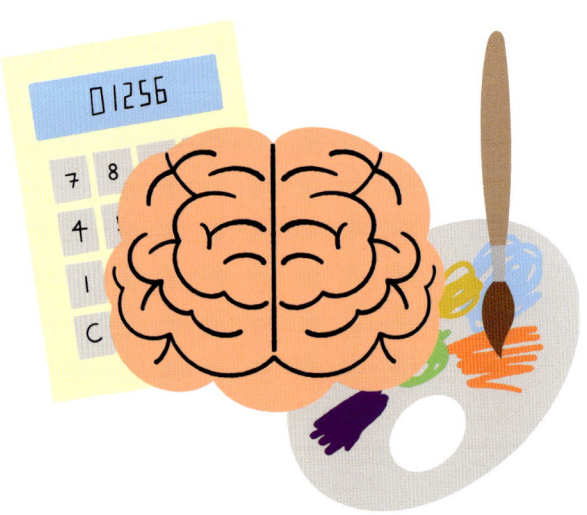

lateralization

Sometimes referred to as 'hemispheric dominance', lateralization is also inaccurately used as a synonym for left-brain, right-brain dominance, but there are key differences. Lateralization refers to the tendency of certain functions to be specialized on one side of the brain or the other. Although the macrostructure of the brain hemispheres looks identical on the outside, there are different neuronal networks distributed in each side. This means that each side does indeed have distinct capabilities.

Brain laterality is about the location of functional elements across both sides of the brains of humans and animals. This is usually asymmetric. Humans have five lateralized functions: handedness (which hand you favour for certain tasks), language ability, spatial skills, facial recognition and emotional recognition. Crucially, lateralization is unique to individuals, as our brains all develop differently, and there are counter-examples for every generalization.

The best examples of established lateralization are those of Broca's area (named after the physician who discovered this in the 1860s), which is concerned with language production, and Wernicke's area (ditto), concerned with language comprehension. Both are usually found exclusively on the left hemisphere of the brain. Yet, functions like intonation or accentuation are generally thought to occur in neurons on both hemispheres. It is not a simple case of left or right controlling one function; it is complex and there is much still to be discovered.

In a nutshell
The theory that functions in the brain occur in different regions in each hemisphere of the brain.

Why it matters
This helps researchers understand which parts of the brain are more or less responsible for which actions and thought processes. It has implications for brain health and for those with brain injuries.

Key figures
Joseph Bogen, 1926–2005
Norman Geschwind, 1926–1984
Brenda Milner, b.1918

Make the connection
synesthaesia/colour blindness, pp.52–3
amnesia, p.98
psychiatric medication, p.103

brain scans

A brain scan is a painless test that produces clear images of the structures inside your head.

Magnetic resonance imaging (MRI) is a specific type of scanning that uses magnetic fields and radio waves to produce detailed images of the structure of the brain in real time. Since the technique's invention in around 1971, theories of brain functioning have expanded rapidly, as MRI allows us to see and analyse brain activity,.

Functional magnetic resonance imaging (fMRI) is slightly different. MRI creates pictures of the inside of the body, while fMRI focuses only on the brain and looks at metabolic activity over time. It measures changes in blood flow and oxygenation associated with our neural activity. This has allowed researchers to identify brain regions involved in specific tasks or mental processes.

There are other types of brain scans. For example, computed tomography (CT) scans take a rapid series of x-ray pictures, which are put together to create images similar (at least to the untrained eye) to those generated by an MRI.

Amazing research studies are now emerging, in which meditating monks or people falling in love have been put under an fMRI scanner to see what is going on inside the brain. One researcher, Charles Limb, placed jazz pianists and rappers inside an MRI machine and had them perform. The imaging showed that the most prolific improvisers manage to shut off those parts of their brains that handle self-monitoring, leading Limb to conclude what many musical improvisers know – they can trust themselves to act instinctively!

In a nutshell
Tools used to help us visualize and understand the structure, connectivity and function of areas of the brain.

Why it matters
Brain scans play a crucial role in advancing knowledge of brain function and structure. They inform diagnosis and intervention to optimize brain health and cognitive functioning.

Key figures
Paul Broca, 1824–1880
Korbinian Brodmann, 1868–1918
Wilder Penfield, 1891–1976

Make the connection
cortex, p.144
lateralization, p.149

electroencephalography

This non-invasive neuroimaging technique is used to measure and record electrical activity generated by the brain's neurons. Like MRI and other brain-scanning techniques, electroencephalography (EEG) helps us examine the workings of the brain and can be used to diagnose neurological disorders like epilepsy, sleep disorders and brain tumours. The process is slightly different, however.

In order to administer EEG, electrodes are placed on the scalp. Once attached, these detect and amplify tiny electrical signals produced by neural firing, which are shown as wavy lines on a screen or printout (an electrogram).

EEG provides a direct, real-time measure of brain activity. Consequently, it is used to encourage biofeedback. For example, if you are experiencing panic, an EEG reading might help to establish a connection between the intensity of the experience and techniques like breathing or challenging your thoughts. EEG feedback is sometimes used for attention deficit hyperactivity disorder (ADHD), pain management, addiction, anxiety and depression.

Researchers also use EEG to study brain rhythms and oscillatory activity associated with different cognitive tasks or experimental manipulations. The trouble with EEG is that its spatial resolution is pretty poor. This means that although it can detect *when* neural activity is happening, unlike MRI, CT or other scanning methods, it cannot detect *where* the activity occurs in the brain.

In a nutshell
An EEG test measures electrical activity in the brain using small metal discs, electrodes, wired to the scalp.

Why it matters
EEG can be useful for diagnosing neurological or mental–health difficulties.

Key figures
Frederick Andermann, 1930–2019
Hans Berger, 1873–1941
Joe Kamiya, 1925–2021

Make the connection
colour blindness, p.53
ADHD, p.93
psychopathy, p.123

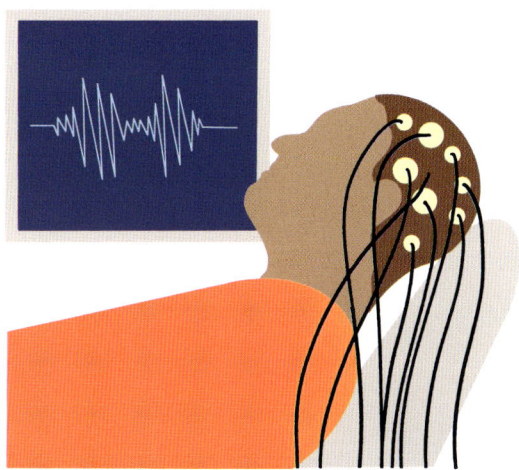

Alzheimer's disease

Alzheimer's disease is a progressive, irreversible brain condition. It primarily affects memory, cognition and behaviour, and ultimately leads to severe impairment in daily functioning and to loss of independence. It is very distressing to witness in our loved ones.

Named after Dr Alois Alzheimer, who first described the condition in 1906, Alzheimer's disease is the most common cause of dementia, accounting for about 70 percent of all cases. A common early symptom is difficulty remembering new information. This may be subtle at first, and may be dismissed as normal forgetting or age-related memory decline. As the disease advances, people have difficulty remembering recent events or finding words, with impaired judgement also a symptom. Psychological symptoms include agitation, aggression and mood changes. We don't know the exact causes of the disease, but several risk factors are widely known: age, genetics and lifestyle factors like cardiovascular health, diet and physical activity.

At the moment there is no cure for Alzheimer's. The available treatments aim to slow the progression of the disease through medications that target neurotransmitter imbalances. Cognitive stimulation programs and support services for carers are also beneficial for sufferers. Research in the area is focused on developing disease modifying therapies that target the underlying mechanisms of the disease.

In a nutshell
A neurodegenerative disorder that affects memory, cognition and behaviour. It ultimately leads to severe impairment and the loss of ability to manage daily life tasks.

Why it matters
The mental and physical effects of Alzheimer's are devastating, so research into its development and possible treatments is a priority.

Key figures
Alois Alzheimer, 1864–1915
John Hardy, b.1954
Rudolph Tanzi, b.1958

Make the connection
memory/forgetting, pp.40–41
cognitive reserve, p.59
amnesia, p.98

Parkinson's disease

Like Alzheimer's, Parkinson's is a progressive neurogenerative disorder, but it looks quite different. It is characterized by motor symptoms such as tremors, slowness of movement (bradykinesia), rigidity and postural instability. The average age of onset is sixty years. Early symptoms of the disease are very subtle – tremors, softness of speech or difficulty getting out of a chair.

Named after Dr James Parkinson, who first described the condition in 1817, Parkinson's disease affects the dopamine-producing neurons in an area of the brain called the substantia nigra region. Dopamine is a neurotransmitter, a chemical messenger. If there is not enough of it in the body, the result is motor dysfunction. On top of motor symptoms, Parkinson's disease can cause problems including impairment in cognition, mood disturbances, difficulties with sleep and other sensory and autonomic system failures.

The biological reason for the differences between the two diseases is that Alzheimer's is characterized by the accumulation on the brain of beta-amyloid plaques – clumps of a naturally occurring protein – that disrupt cell function. Parkinson's is characterized by the loss of dopamine-producing neurons and the formation of Lewy bodies (also clumps of protein particles, but containing a particular protein called alpha-synuclein).

In the West, one of the best-known sufferers from Parkinson's is the actor Michael J. Fox, who was diagnosed with the illness aged twenty-nine and has since advocated tirelessly for research into it.

In a nutshell
A disease of the brain that causes involuntary movement and difficulty with coordination and balance. Symptoms worsen over time.

Why it matters
It is possible for those with Parkinson's disease to have a full and rich life, but it is important to know how it comes on and what we can do to alleviate symptoms.

Key figures
Oleh Hornykiewicz, 1926–2020
William Langston
James Parkinson, 1755–1824

Make the connection
electroencephalo–graphy, p.151
brain, p.155

mind

All of psychology is to do with the mind. After all, the word comes from the Greek words *psych*, meaning mind, soul or spirit, and *logo*, meaning discourse or study. The mind is that which thinks, remembers, perceives or senses. It can experience conscious or unconscious states. It is connected to feelings of pleasure, pain and everything in between. The human mind is the central object of study in psychology, from cognition to memory and mental illness.

Other disciplines, like philosophy, religion and neuroscience, are equally curious about the mind.

Philosophy, for example, considers whether other living organisms have minds. Can they think, feel and learn? And if so, how? Some see the mind as an exclusively human entity, but others support pan-psychism or animism, where properties of the mind are ascribed to other, non-human, even non-animal entities.

Dominant and influential psychological theories of the mind came from figures like Sigmund Freud and Carl Jung (see pp.30, 31), but more surprising are the contributions that computer scientists like Alan Turing have made to the understanding of mind. As technology develops, and our human minds design more of it, theories of the mind are ever-expanding. And now, as we enter the age of AI, there is the possibility of non-biological machinery duplicating the work of the human mind – it's a brave new world.

In a nutshell
A major element of being human – thinking, feeling, perception, consciousness and information-processing.

Why it matters
Study of the mind is the essence of psychology. Other disciplines – philosophy and religion – also pay attention to its purpose and functions.

Key figures
René Descartes, 1596–1650
William James, 1842–1910
Karl Popper, 1902–1994

Make the connection
dreaming, p.12
hallucinations, p.63
consciousness/the unconscious, pp.146–7

brain

Whereas the term 'mind' refers to your ability to think, feel and engage in complex human activities, the brain is the actual physical organ in your skull that makes it all happen. The brain *activates* behaviours, thinking and, in fact, all mental and physical processes. The mind is the *experience* of these processes, but none of it would happen without the brain engine whirring away in the background.

Neuropsychology focuses on the structure, development and function of the brain, including the spinal cord. Our brains and spinal cords are packed with neurons. These are nerve cells that send messages all over our bodies, allowing us to do everything from breathing to sleeping, crying to completing that crossword. As the name suggests, sensory neurons carry information that we experience though touch, smell, sight, sound and taste. Other neurons, like motor neurons, transmit information from the brain to the muscles and glands of the body.

Until recently, most neuroscientists thought that we were born with all the neurons we were ever going to have over the course of a lifetime. Lately, however, they have found that, through the process of neuroplasticity, whereby our nerve cells grow and reorganize, new neurons are developing at all ages and stages of life. Neurons respond sensitively and simultaneously to outside information and join up in many ways.

It is an enormous job for a relatively small piece of the body!

In a nutshell
A complex organ that controls memory, emotion, senses, breathing and every other process that regulates the body.

Why it matters
The study of the brain can shed light on the interaction between biology and psychology, helping us to understand the overlap between brain, mind and behaviours.

Key figures
Paul Broca, 1824–1880
Roger Sperry, 1913–1994
Carl Wernicke, 1848–1905

Make the connection
neuroplasticity, p.27
lateralization, p.149
brain scans, p.150

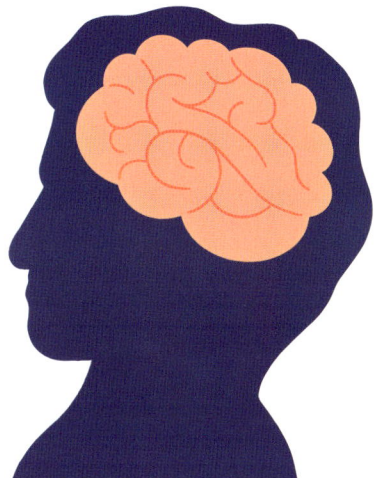

movers & shakers

The following, highly selective list highlights 20 key figures currently working in the field of psychology. These are the 'movers and shakers' reshaping this millennia-old discipline.

Tara Brach (b.1953) is an American psychologist, author and meditation teacher, whose work blends Buddhist teaching, specifically the practices of meditation and mindfulness, with Western psychological practice. Her books and podcast reach a wide audience.

James Clear (b.1986) has a background in performance coaching and public speaking. In his 2018 best-seller, *Atomic Habits*, which draws on behavioural psychology among other fields of knowledge, he argues that it is possible to live a better life by adopting better habits – as he puts it, by getting '1% better everyday'.

Carole Dweck (b.1946) popularized the concept of the growth mindset in her 2006 book *Mindset: The New Psychology of Success*. She continues to research and publish in this area and in the wider field of 'motivation', which she considers to bridge the areas of developmental, social and personality psychology.

Peter Fonagy (b.1952) is a giant of modern psychology, with a special interest in the fields of early attachment relationships, social cognition and borderline personality disorder. He is the innovator of Mentalization-Based Treatment (MBT), a research-based therapeutic approach that aims to improve the patient's ability to 'mentalize', or conceive of, their emotional states.

Uta Frith (b.1941) is a pioneer of autism and dyslexia research, whose work has focussed on the neurological basis of these conditions. As a distinguished psychologist and neuroscientist herself, she advocates for the advancement of women in science.

Jonathan Haidt (b.1963) works in the fields of moral and social psychology, especially the study of moral reasoning and 'moral emotions' In recent years he has become a prominent voice promoting political civility and intellectual diversity, aiming to reduce what he sees as increased political polarization.

Claudia Hammond (b.1971) is a British broadcaster and journalist. Her interest lies in communicating innovations in psychology, mental health and neuroscience to a popular audience. She presents BBC radio show *All in the Mind*, among others.

Janet Helms is an American research psychologist, well known for her work on racial identity and the phenomenon of racial biases in cognitive ability tests and measurements. Her 1992 book *A Race is a Nice Thing to Have*, which looks at white racial identity, is one of over 100 publications bearing her name.

Lucy Johnstone is a critical voice in clinical psychology practice, of which she is a veteran, drawing our attention to the need for compassionate, patient-oriented approaches that ask not 'what's wrong with you?', but 'what happened to you?' (a simple definition of trauma-informed practice, or TIP).

Marsha Linehan (b.1943) developed dialectical behaviour therapy (DBT), a psychotherapeutic treatment for borderline personality disorder, partly as a result of her own experience with mental illness. She is considered an innovator in mental health practice and is also a Zen meditation teacher.

Elizabeth Loftus (b.1944) is best known for her work on false memory and misinformation, and has made high-profile appearances as an expert witness in a number of legal trials. She is a vocal critic of 'recovered memory' therapy, arguing that human memory is extremely fallible and liable to distortion.

Eleanor Longden describes the process of making peace with the voices she hears as putting an end to 'internal civil war'. A psychology academic, she is best known for a 2012 TED talk in which she discusses her schizophrenia diagnosis and the positive impact on her life of the UK 'Hearing Voices Network'.

David Nutt (b.1951) is a British neuropsychopharmacologist and a prominent commentator on drugs and drug use. His non-profit, Drug Science, provides independent, evidence-based information on drugs and campaigns for evidence-based drugs policy. Nutt is at the forefront of research into the use of psychedelics in clinical practice.

Elizabeth Peel is a social psychologist based at Loughborough University, UK, with particular interests in (non-heterosexual) sexualities and health communication relating to patients with dementia. She is co-editor of the 'Gender and Sexualities in Psychology' book series, and an advocate for qualitative research methods in psychology.

Steven Pinker (b.1954) is the author of both popular and academic books on psychology, with a particular emphasis on language – how we learn it, think it and what it means to use it (in his view, that we are inherently linguistic animals, with an ever-evolving skill for communicating).

Allan Schore (b.1943) is an American neuropsychologist and practising psychotherapist. His work integrates attachment theory with neuroscience, exploring the connections between, for example, early attachment trauma and brain development, and the implications of both for the capacity to regulate emotion.

Martin Seligman (b.1942) is the author of numerous books on positive psychology, as well as *Character Strengths and Virtues* (2004), a kind of counterpart or mirror to the DSM that lists six key trans-historical virtues. His concept of 'learned helplessness' has been highly influential in clinical psychology.

Mark Solms (b.1961) is a prominent figure in neuropsychoanalysis, exploring the connections between our knowledge of the brain and our experiences of behaviour and cognition. His 1997 book on the neuropsychology of dreams is considered a landmark in the field, and more popular works include *The Brain and the Inner World* (2002).

Mark Williams (b.1952) was founding director of the Oxford Mindfulness Centre and is co-author of *Mindfulness: A Practical Guide to Finding Peace in a Frantic World* (2011), which aims to bring the theory of mindfulness-based cognitive therapy (MBCT) to a wider audience. This therapeutic approach was co-developed by Williams in the course of his work on depression and suicide prevention.

Richard Wiseman (b.1966) has published over 100 academic papers examining the psychology of magic, illusion, deception, luck and self-development. An ex-magician himself, he has a particular interest in the psychology of performance and also public engagement.

index

IVY PRESS

**First published in 2025 by Ivy Press
an imprint of The Quarto Group.**

One Triptych Place, London, SE1 9SH, United Kingdom
T (0)20 7700 6700
www.Quarto.com

A catalogue record for this book is available from the British Library.

ISBN 978-0-71129-884-2
Ebook ISBN 978-0-71129-885-9

Design by Intercity
Editor Faye Robson
Production Manager Rohana Yusof
Series Editor Jane Wilsher
We would like to extend our thanks to Guntaas Kaur
Chugh for providing an inclusivity read on the book.

Printed in China
10 9 8 7 6 5 4 3 2 1